Flickers of History

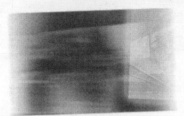

Flickers of History

A newsreel cameraman's story

WILLIAM CARTY with Gabrielle Chan

To Sue & Jack,

With fond memories to our Dear friends of the 8th army. In my war career, Jack you were the nicest P.R. of them all. Sorry we didn't see much of Sue.

1st June have been invited up to Japan, God willing. 2 days in Tokyo & 3 days in Nara. Jim will be going up with us. God Bless you both – Keep well – Hope you enjoy the book –

HarperCollinsPublishers

Warmest regards to you both –
Mary & Bill Carty – 1999 –

HarperCollins*Publishers*

First published in Australia in 1999
by HarperCollins*Publishers* Pty Limited
ACN 009 913 517
A member of the HarperCollins*Publishers* (Australia) Pty Limited Group
http://www.harpercollins.com.au

Copyright © William M. Carty 1999

This book is copyright.
Apart from any fair dealing for the purposes of private study, research, criticism or review, as permitted under the Copyright Act, no part may be reproduced by any process without written permission.
Inquiries should be addressed to the publishers.

HarperCollins*Publishers*
25 Ryde Road, Pymble, Sydney, NSW 2073, Australia
31 View Road, Glenfield, Auckland 10, New Zealand
77–85 Fulham Palace Road, London W6 8JB, United Kingdom
Hazelton Lanes, 55 Avenue Road, Suite 2900, Toronto, Ontario M5R 3L2
and 1995 Markham Road, Scarborough, Ontario M1B 5M8, Canada
10 East 53rd Street, New York NY 10022, USA

National Library of Australia Cataloguing-in-Publication data:

Carty, William M.
 Flickering history.
 ISBN 0 7322 6738 2.
 1. Carty, William M. 2. War photographers – Australia –
 Biography. 3. News photographers – Australia – Biography.
 4. World War, 1939–1945 – Personal narratives, Australian.
 5. World War, 1939–1945 – Campaigns – Pacific Ocean.
 6. World War, 1939–1945 – Motion pictures and the war.
 I. Chan, Gabrielle. II. Title.
940.5426

Cover photographs: (front, left to right) Australasian Films Studio, Rushcutters Bay, 1923; Bill Carty, film cameraman, about to take off in a Piper Cub on a spotting mission to direct the shelling of heavy artillery on Noemfor Island; Bill Carty in Japan with his new Bell & Howell camera, bought by the Newsreel pool for the occupation of Japan and the Far East; (back) Bill Carty in military uniform.

Printed in Australia by Griffin Press Pty Ltd on 70gsm Ensobelle

9 8 7 6 5 4 3 2 1
02 01 00 99

Dedicated to my wife
Mary Margaret Carty
for her patience and support

and our children

Helen Margaret Carty
James Patrick Carty
Pauline Therese Gallagher
Patricia Ann Gallagher

Acknowledgments

THIS BOOK HAS been a long time in the making, as you will see from General Eichelberger's foreword, written in 1949. I would like to express my profound thanks to the following people, without whose help these memoirs would not have been possible: Margaret Walker, Louise, Madeleine and Siobhan Gallagher, Patricia Murphy and Marion Leake, who were all invaluable in helping to prepare the manuscript.

I also gratefully acknowledge those photographers whose wonderful photos helped illustrate my story. There are also many photographers who remain anonymous. My sincere thanks to the following who supplied photos, including:

Nimitz Museum, Fredericksburg, Texas
US Navy
US Army
US Signal Corps
Eighth Army Photographic Unit
Australian Sound and Film Archive
MacArthur Memorial, Virginia
ACME Pictures
Associated Press
United Press
US International News Service
US National Archives & Records Administration
Australian Government Department of Information

This book is a collection of my memories of events, as I saw them or as told to me by friends and colleagues. Some of the details may differ from the accounts of others, but, to my knowledge, they are correct.

Bill Carty

I would like to thank Jennifer Chan, Janet Murray and Richard Littlejohn for their assistance and suggestions. It would have been an impossible task without the support of my husband, Richard Hart.

Gabrielle Chan

Contents

Foreword by Robert Eichelberger — xi

PART I: Flickers — 1

Chapter One: Horse and cart days — 3
Chapter Two: Flickers — 21
Chapter Three: America — 33

PART II: War — 53

Chapter Four: Call-up — 55
Chapter Five: Action — 69
Chapter Six: The Carty luck — 83
Chapter Seven: Chaplains — 97
Chapter Eight: Paramount — 105
Chapter Nine: Surrender — 113

PART III: Occupation — 131

Chapter Ten: Devastation — 133
Chapter Eleven: War crimes — 143
Chapter Twelve: The emperor — 155
Chapter Thirteen: Family business — 167
Chapter Fourteen: Generals — 181
Chapter Fifteen: The Japanese — 195
Chapter Sixteen: Far East — 211
Chapter Seventeen: Farewell — 221

Epilogue — 229

Foreword

BILL CARTY IS one of a small handful of gallant newsmen who stuck it out with us at Buna and told the world in pictures of that first bloody ground victory over the Japanese in which American forces were involved. To my mind, no story of the war in the Pacific is complete without an authentic account of that first turning of the tide. Such an account cannot be written second-hand by an historian. Bill Carty can write it because he witnessed it with us.

Bill was part of a great group of Australian correspondents who followed the Allies northward from Australia. Of all these fine men, Bill, with his flashing smile and his ready camera, was one of the best known and best loved.

Too many people, I believe, have forgotten Buna, Gona and Sanananda. The last stage of a war is always the most dramatic, and the Second World War is no exception: the Philippines, Okinawa, the B-29 attacks on Japan, the truly awful advent of the atomic bomb, and, finally, our occupation of Japan itself will remain vividly in our minds for a long time. But to those of us who were there, the battles in New Guinea – some of the bloodiest of the Pacific War – were the foundation on which our ultimate victory was laid.

It is hard to believe now that we fought and won with so little in those early days. The US 32nd Division, the Australian 7th Division, the Australian 18th Brigade, the Royal Australian Air Force and the Royal Australian Navy started with little and wound up with a good deal less. There were no replacements in those days. There were no jungle veterans among us because this was the first jungle we had ever seen. There was little equipment, little food, little of anything except courage, determination and sheer will to win. The Americans and the Australians won a war at Buna in January 1943. The Japanese were beaten at their own jungle game – decisively beaten and driven back. They were beaten not because we had superior equipment. We didn't. They were beaten because the American doughboy and the Aussie digger proved to be better men.

Bill and his fine family did much to promote the lasting friendship between the Yanks and the Aussies in Japan. To Bill Carty and those other war correspondents who lived with us through those incredible days, Americans might pay heed. Their stories are the lessons of preparedness – the fabric of a hard-won peace. They are stories to be read and pondered by all of us. Bill Carty saw a great deal of General Douglas MacArthur, and his book should be of particular interest to those who helped bring victory to the Pacific.

Robert L. Eichelberger,
retired lieutenant general, USA, Yokohama, Japan,
October 1949

Right: Bill Carty at sixteen years of age. Bill shot his first story in 1924 on this silent film camera.

Left: 'The girl in the cute hat.' Mary Margaret Murphy agreed to marry Bill Carty in 1934.

A portrait of the Carty family taken in 1908. Daisy and Patrick Carty, Bill's parents, are in the second front row, third and fourth from the left.

Part I

Flickers

Walter Sully, Australasian Films Studio's chief newsreel cameraman, gave Bill his first job. In this picture Wally is skating around the parapet of the Commonwealth Bank in Martin Place, Sydney.

Chapter One

Horse and cart days

The Carty family in 1911: Kathleen Louise (aged 2), Patrick , Bill (aged 3), and Daisy.

IT WAS TWILIGHT in a Sydney summer. The cicadas shrilled, and inside our tiny Paddington terrace my family waited for the southerly to cool us down. I had just brushed my teeth and was ready for bed. Lingering in the front yard, I waited for Mum to call me in. Suddenly, a flickering light overflowed onto the road down the hill. As I walked slowly to the front gate, the sound of the family clearing up the dinner dishes faded. The light was coming from the oval at the bottom of Cascade Street and was irresistible to a five-year-old boy.

Flickers of History

The magical light filled the night sky. It illuminated the summer insects and threw strange shapes as far as Glenmore Road. Spellbound, I wandered out the front gate then accelerated down the steep hill to Hampden Oval (now Trumper Park). A large truck parked in the middle of the oval held a machine that projected a series of moving pictures onto a large wide screen. There was no sound from the screen, only the cheers, laughs and hisses of the appreciative audience. I joined the crowd and was enchanted by the people on the screen who towered over me. My eyes felt like they would explode: the image was so different to anything I had ever experienced. I was hypnotised, until a hand fell onto my shoulder from behind. 'What are you doing here, kid? Can't remember you paying.'

My parents arrived just minutes after my capture. They were frantic, of course, but guessed from the open front gate and the far-off flickering light that I could be nowhere else. My mother grabbed me, giving me a hug and a shake simultaneously. 'Don't ever run off like that again,' she roused. I didn't hear the rest. I was still watching the screen. Most of the audience was in love with the stars. I was in love with the medium.

My grandparents, William Carty and Mary Boylen, were born in County Clare, Ireland, on the eve of the potato famine. The total failure at the potato crop between 1845 and 1848 meant Ireland starved. It was a desperate time for the Cartys and the Boylens. Accompanying the famine was the ever-present threat of diseases, such as scurvy, dysentery and yellow fever. Later, as teenagers, William and Mary dreamed of moving to a country where they could make a living and raise a family in less uncertain circumstances.

The famine had already driven thousands of people to North America, where they hoped to find a better life. Almost one and a half million people emigrated in the 1840s. There were tearful farewells on the docks as families realised they might not see their young ones again. Years later, William and Mary told their parents of their plan to emigrate, prompting long and painful discussions. Although their parents put up a fight, they knew in their hearts that leaving Ireland would provide their children with a better future.

In 1872 William made the break first, arriving in Bradford, England, where he got a job in the building trade. Mary arrived shortly afterwards and found work in a dressmaking business. They lived two blocks from each other, and, to no one's surprise, it wasn't long before the childhood sweethearts were engaged. On 30 September 1873, they were married in St Patrick's Church in Bradford.

The Cartys were expecting their first child when they started considering the United States or Australia as their ultimate destination. Although they had found work quickly in England, it failed to meet their expectations. The Irish were treated badly and it felt too much like the same old world, the world they had tried to escape. On the other hand, they had heard promising tales from the colony of New South Wales. They decided to apply to emigrate to Australia. Their first child, Patrick, was six weeks old when they left England.

Flickers of History

The only way to reach their new home was by sailing ship. It was a voyage they would never forget. Fresh water was for drinking, salt water for bathing. The passengers survived on salted beef and meat from animals slaughtered on the journey. Sleeping quarters, particularly for the second-class and third-class passengers, were primitive. Almost everyone suffered from seasickness. William and Mary tried desperately to comfort little Patrick in the cramped conditions. Despite the ordeal, he survived and was almost eight months when they again stood on firm ground.

William and Mary settled in Paddington in Sydney. A builder and plasterer by trade, William set about building a home in Glenmore Road to house what would be a large family. The five-bedroom house still stands today, with the same solid oak front door.

My maternal grandfather, John Moore, was born in England, but, as soon as he was old enough, set sail for Australia. John decided Sydney's city life, such as it was in the 1800s, was not for him, and he headed west to Dubbo in New South Wales. He opened his doors as a tailor and met and married a country girl, Elizabeth Miller. They had five boys – John, Harold, Stanley, Wilfred and Leo – and three girls – Violet, Daisy and Ivy. Death came early to the Moore family: Violet and Stanley died in their youth, and their father, John, died at forty-eight, leaving Elizabeth to rear six young children. Daisy was six when her father died, and Ivy and Leo barely knew him.

It was a difficult time for the young mother, who took in washing and cleaned houses to earn enough to raise a large family. Elizabeth thought it might be easier for her family in Sydney, so she rented a house in Elizabeth Street, Paddington. When the boys turned fourteen, they left school to work. Their sister Daisy followed them, and for a short time she helped her mother clean houses. By sixteen she was a striking brunette. She joined a chorus line on the stage in Sydney, where she worked for Bland Holt, one of the top theatre managers of the time.

Daisy Moore met Patrick Carty a year after her appearance on the stage and their relationship caused a stir from the beginning. In the first place, Patrick, as the eldest son, was required to support his family by handing his pay-packet to his mother at the end of each week, as was the custom in Ireland. His decision to leave home and marry upset his parents. But it was Daisy's religion that caused the biggest problem: she was a strict Protestant while the Cartys were Catholics. Their prospective union would be a 'mixed marriage', sure to bring condemnation from both sides. Sectarianism was widespread in Australia, as new migrants brought their old hatreds and fears from the countries of their birth. Companies employed people according to their religious persuasion. For example, one of Sydney's landmark department stores, Mark Foy's, only employed Catholics. Although Daisy and Patrick were unaware at the time, theirs was not the first mixed marriage in the Moore family. Daisy's grandfather was Jewish, a secret not revealed until the 1960s.

In 1907, when Daisy turned eighteen, she married Patrick in St Mary's Cathedral, a beautiful sandstone Catholic church in central Sydney. The ceremony had to be conducted behind the main altar because of Daisy's religion. If frightened or in the least bit apprehensive, or even overjoyed, the couple could not look to the pews for support, for no one from either family came. They had been abandoned by those closest to them, and neither side would relent for the rest of their lives. The Carty family never met the Moore family.

I was born on 9 February 1908, in our house at Union Street, Paddington, near both the Cartys and the Moores. Grandma Carty walked past our house every day for two years without dropping in to see me or her son. My grandfather, William Carty, had died just a month before I was born, so I did not meet either grandfather. I was left with two cold grandmothers, a situation I never understood. Grandma Carty, in particular, never showed any curiosity about her grandchildren, let alone any affection for her own children. As we grew up, she allowed us to visit her house in Rushcutters Bay. She dressed in black and always sat in the kitchen next to the wood stove, even on the hottest summer day. To me, she looked as though she were a hundred years old. Even when we visited, she never gave us so much as a peck on the cheek. Yet when she died, my mother was the one who laid her out.

My sister Kathleen was born more than a year after me, and, despite the cool relationship, we moved in with Grandma Moore in Elizabeth Street, Paddington. We all lived in the front room, the only one in the terrace with a balcony. Mum's two brothers lived in the house and Grandma rented out a room downstairs to bring in some extra money. Mum and Grandma shared the cooking for all of us.

It was in this kitchen that a doctor removed my mother's tonsils, using local anaesthetic. I wasn't allowed in to see the

Part I: Flickers

operation, but she immediately got up and cooked us all a hot dinner. As the anaesthetic wore off, I became terrified: my mother went crazy, writhing with the pain. It was an experience that haunted me when, at the age of six, I had my own tonsils removed.

A short woman with fair hair, Grandma Moore, despite never showing us any affection, was a good and quietly spoken woman. Sadly, she never warmed to us. Of course, being Catholic didn't help us much. Maybe in an effort to turn us around, she took us to her own Protestant church service on Sundays in the front room of a hall in Sutherland Street. There the owner, Mrs Murray, gave us a holy picture and told us bible stories. I enjoyed the outing because there were other kids from the area, and Dad didn't seem to mind at all. By the time I was five, we had moved to Cascade Street, near the Chinese market gardens in Paddington, and that was the end of Mrs Murray's instruction.

These were the days of the horse and cart. Australia was like a sleepy hollow, particularly before the First World War. I feel incredibly lucky to have lived through those times. My favourite spot to sleep was the veranda on the front of the house, in the cool air. If it rained, I would simply pull the covers over my head, even if the bed was soaking wet. Invariably, Mum would order me inside. From my veranda, I could listen to the passing parade.

At night there was the clip-clop of the horse that pulled the milk cart. The rattle of the metal as the milko poured his milk

Flickers of History

into our cans was music to my ears. He carried the containers to our front door and measured a pint or quart into a can, leaving it on the doorstep. Mum could collect it anytime after 4 am. Although the cans were usually covered, if it rained the milko nearly always left the covers off. It was like a bad joke.

Bread was also delivered by horse and cart. A man would knock on the door holding a basketful of loaves, covered with a piece of cloth. The homely smell of the bread filled the neighbourhood. Then there was a host of other callers tramping the streets with their wares. A regular caller was a man yelling 'clothes props, get your clothes props'. They sold for one shilling and sixpence. The 'rabbito' man carried a chopper and a sharp knife. For nine pence, he would skin and clean a rabbit on the back of his cart, surrounded by a cloud of flies. The fisherman came on Fridays – no ice, just fresh fish, scaled and cleaned on your doorstep. Prawns were sold by the pint – again one shilling and sixpence.

At the end of the day, I watched as the gas lamps were lit to illuminate the streets. Each was the traditional lamppost, with glass enclosing a burner and mantle that was ignited using a long pole with a hook on the end. A man pulled a small ring on the end of a chain, which would ignite the burner. In the dead of night, these lamps failed to throw much light. You had to stand directly beneath them to see your hand in front of your face. Inside our house, the lights were not much better. We used candles and kerosene lamps, which we carried from room to room. There was only one gas jet burning in the kitchen at night to light the lamps. Not that we needed lighting for long: most people who were home were in bed by 9 pm.

Part I: Flickers

Apart from the travelling salesmen, the corner grocery store was one of the only local places to buy food. The grocer opened five and a half days a week and usually retired with a small fortune. He ran a book for each customer, totting up items through the week. Saturday was for settling up.

The market garden also supplied the area with fresh vegetables. The garden was tended by Chinese workers, who carried buckets of water on the end of bamboo poles laid along their shoulders. In this way, they irrigated the whole of the gardens. Good customers would receive a jar of Chinese preserved ginger.

Sunday was traditionally the day of rest, although we spent most of our time running around doing anything but resting. Like mothers all around Australia, Mum cooked a roast dinner of lamb, beef, veal, or sometimes pork in a fuel stove, even on the hottest days of summer. The smell wafted out the window and filled the street. Somehow, roasts never smelled as good in an electric stove.

It was against the law for shopkeepers to trade on Sundays, so the shops were closed – unless you knew someone. The proprietors waited behind closed shopfronts for the knock on the door. When the knock came, the shopkeeper opened the door enough to peer through. If he did not recognise you, the door closed in your face. If he knew you, the door opened wide enough for him to glance both ways before he pulled you into the safety of his premises. You then had to go through the same charade on the way out: secretive glances were made out the barely ajar door, and, if the coast was clear, you were pushed unceremoniously onto the street and the door slammed shut

Flickers of History

behind you. Of course, all police were on foot then. There were no patrol cars, which was probably an advantage for the vigilant cop waiting for a Sunday seller. Walking the streets, he could watch the doors and the window shoppers closely and impose a heavy fine on wilful shopkeepers.

You could get a milkshake at the beaches at weekends because milk bars were allowed to stay open until 11 pm on Saturday and Sunday. These shops became meeting places for the teenagers along the beaches, and our spot was Pal's milk bar on Bondi Beach, opposite the Casino dance hall. My standard order was a strawberry milkshake and toast.

School started at five years for everyone except me. I came down with a serious bout of pneumonia, delaying a rather unremarkable school career by two years. Mum and Dad thought they were going to lose me. I felt like someone had tied a belt around my chest, tightened to the last notch. I couldn't breathe properly, but the doctors didn't seem to know what to do. They gave my mother numerous prescriptions, which we had filled in a little alcove on Oxford Street, Paddington.

I was seven before I was introduced to the terrifying world of nuns, canes and arithmetic at St Joseph's School in Woollahra. Those nuns were tough old birds. Sister Imelda, who was later to convert my mother as she worked on the school fêtes, showed a different side of her character in the classroom. She would chase the kids around, waving a bamboo cane. Frightened children hid under desks to get away from her. Once she grabbed me by the ears, although I could never understand what I had done wrong. I was too frightened of her cane to ever really be naughty.

I was not a great success at school. Sister Imelda hammered the times tables into me, but it did little good. As far as arithmetic was concerned, I was buggered. I liked geography, but that was not going to get me far – or so I thought.

The nuns may have been cruel in the classroom, but nothing could rival the cruelty of the kids in the playground. Everyone was picked on for some fault. One boy, who had a strangely shaped head, was known as Seven Heads. They wouldn't leave him alone. Long after we left school I saw him across the bar in a pub, but I didn't strike up a conversation. What could I say to Seven Heads?

For all the terror and teasing, school did not interfere much with my life, for I divided all my spare time between the beach and the pictures. We swam at our own risk in those days. None of the beaches was protected by nets, and the harbour, in particular, was infested with sharks. Those who swam at Balmoral, Manly, Watsons Bay and Nielsen Park (called Shark Beach) were all regularly warned of the danger.

Dad used to take me down to Rushcutters Bay. There was no surf there, but it was close to home. The bay had two swimming pools, known as baths. Men and women swam separately, as mixed bathing was not allowed. On the beach, women wore neck-to-knee cotton swim dresses with stockings, while the men wore full cotton swimsuits. When I was as young as two, Dad would put me on the diving board at the swimming pool, where I would balance precariously before jumping off into his arms.

Dad also swam in the open water regularly. One day he noticed a man throwing a stick for his fox terrier to retrieve. The dog bounded in, swimming into the same area as my father, but, as the terrier was about to grab the stick, he disappeared in a silent swirl. A shark had taken the poor creature. Dad rushed out of the water, never to swim there again.

We moved to Bondi when I was nine, and from that time onwards I went to the beach every day after school. I was not a great swimmer – I could not get the breathing right – but I spent a lot of time right out the back in the surf, catching the waves into the shore. The rest of my time was spent doing a lot of silly things to get attention. We built human pyramids, lining the boys up against a wall and kneeling on each other's backs so that the ones on the highest levels were twelve feet up before they crashed into a heap on the ground. Older boys brought their ukuleles down to the beach to play the latest tunes, with varying degrees of success. I was mad about the ukulele, and listened to them play for hours. On Saturdays, I delivered groceries for two shillings for the morning. The shop owner had asked my mother if I would work, and I was happy to earn the pocket-money. I had a trolley made and soon knew all the streets of Bondi.

The year was punctuated with festivals and celebrations and I can't remember ever being bored – we just made our own fun. St Patrick's Day was a big one for the Irish, with running races and Irish dancing. New Year's Day was the main event for the Scots, who tossed the caber at the Sydney Showground.

The Royal Easter Show, the premiere agricultural event, was also a great attraction, and people poured through the streets of Paddington to get to the Showground over the long weekend.

In summer, we could also visit White City, a fun-park built on the site of the Chinese market garden in Rushcutters Bay. An entrepreneur built the park around the largest roller-coaster in Australia, with carriages that traversed a mountain of artificial snow and tore around the tight corners, bringing screams of fear and delight from their passengers. Those not game to try the big dipper took a ride through the river caves or gawked at the midgets from Germany. There was also a hall of mirrors, trapeze artists, and a bearded lady. A highwire walker named Blondin had an act in which he cooked pancakes at the top of his pole before tossing them to the audience below. The sight of the park at night drew people to sit outside the fence just to watch. I was too young to go there alone, but my mother took us there occasionally. Much to my disappointment, she refused to ride on the big dipper, so I missed out on the chief attraction.

Exhilarated by the success of a few summer seasons, the owner decided to open all year round. But those who took the opportunity to wander out on warm summer nights were not interested in going out after dark for much of the rest of the year. White City went broke, and the owner moved on to try his hand in the dance hall business. The fun park was pulled down, and the White City tennis courts took its place in late 1921. The courts boomed, as Australian tennis hit its peak in the 1920s and 1930s, and the New South Wales Tennis Association is still there.

Flickers of History

Friday and Saturday nights were the big nights for balls, when the dance halls were alive until midnight. One of the most popular venues was the Palais Royal at the Showground, but the major department stores in the city, such as Mark Foy's, David Jones and Grace Brothers, hired out their halls regularly.

In winter, when the beach had less appeal, football became the main drawcard. My father recalls an historic meeting that changed football forever. Dad was a keen union player, and a meeting had been called to discuss the change from rugby union to rugby league. League had been played by professionals in England, while union footballers had, apparently, played for the love of it. Dad went down to Hampden Oval to attend the meeting. Australia's greatest player, Dally Messenger, was there, as well as the famous cricketer Victor Trumper. Those present voted to establish a rugby league competition, which had in its charter measures to protect the players from the expense of injury and the risk of permanent loss of employment.

Sports like tennis, soccer and baseball were played all year round. Every weekend, people crowded onto the harbour ferries to watch the yacht races, especially the eighteen-footers with heavy timber hulls and weighty canvas sails. On board every ferry there were bookmakers. Gambling on the races was illegal, but thousands of pounds nevertheless changed hands between excited fans. We would run down to Rushcutters Bay to watch the boats preparing for their weekend racing. Sailing boats of all sizes filled the bay, but it was the eighteen-footers that attracted us most.

Rushcutters Bay was also the site of the first stadium, built by Hugh D. McIntosh, a boxing entrepreneur. It was an open-air stadium, situated next to a huge gasometer and close to Spencer's Studio, which later became Australasian Film Studios. At that time, the world heavyweight champion was the Canadian boxer Tommy Burns. A black American named Jack Johnson wanted to fight him, but the Americans would not allow black men to box in the world title in the United States. McIntosh attracted Burns and Johnson to Australia for a match at his stadium.

Billed as the 'Fight of the Century', 20 000 people crammed into the stadium. The audience included the future prime minister, Billy Hughes, the famous writer Jack London and his wife Charmian (even though women were officially banned from boxing matches), and my father. It was the only fight in Australia that drew such a large crowd. Dad said most of the audience barracked for the white man, but there was no contest. Johnson won after police stopped the fight in the twelfth round.

Australia was as sports crazy then as it is today. Before I turned six, I would sit on the front step in Paddington to ask every passer-by for cigarette cards. Cigarettes were sixpence a pack, and each pack carried a picture card of a famous sports star. The swimmer Dick Cavill, master of the Australian crawl, had a card. He trained regularly down at the old Farmer's Baths in Rushcutters Bay. Then there was Dally Messenger, the footballer, and Les Darcy, Australia's greatest fighter. Fanny Durack, Australia's first female Olympic gold medallist swimmer, also had her own card.

Flickers of History

Once I had established myself with the passing parade of smokers, I gathered quite a pile of cards. One of my regulars was a young man, a chain-smoker, who saved his cards for me and knocked on the front door to give them to my mother if I was not on my step. His name was Walter Sully and he was a newsreel cameraman for Spencer's Studio. He was to provide the door to my career – before he died of emphysema.

Although I did not realise it at the time, money was always a problem for my parents. Dad worked every day of his life for the postmaster, which never brought in a lot of cash. Most of the kids at my school came from similar backgrounds. One boy came from a family of eleven, and they were starving most of the time. But when his father, a tram driver, worked through a strike to earn money to keep his kids, he was derided as a scab, and his children suffered at school.

Like many working-class Catholics, Dad was a deadset Labor man. He constantly talked politics at the dinner table, and Mum agreed, outwardly at least, with his political views. He often turned up to hear politicians spruik on street corners. Apart from the newspapers that was the only place where you could find out their views. One bloke Dad listened to in the early days was Billy Hughes, who was later expelled from the Labor Party over the issue of conscription in the First World War. Hughes became known as Labor's biggest 'rat', which, in Australian terms, means a serious traitor.

When I was about sixteen, Mum noticed an advertisement in the newspaper for someone to temporarily mind a baby boy.

Part I: Flickers

The boy's mother offered pretty good money for the right family, so Mum, always alert for new ways to make ends meet, rang the woman. Arrangements were made, and the little boy, called Ralph, came to live with us. Mum was glad of the extra money. Everything was fine for the first four weeks, but, after that, the money dried up. The mother disappeared, leaving baby Ralph with us. Suddenly, the moneymaking venture started costing my parents dearly.

Mum had been told the name of Ralph's father, though I never found out what it was. He was a tall, lanky grazier, who owned lots of land out west, stocked with sheep and cattle. He was married with a family, but had fathered his maid's child. Mum got in touch with him quite easily, as he spent a fair bit of time in Sydney. She paid him a visit to try to get some money for his son's upkeep, but had no luck. Whether he had paid the mother for his child's keep already, or whether he had simply refused to pay, he never told my mother. He did, however, tell her she had nice legs – that was the extent of his interest. Dad was ropeable. He wanted to track him down and whack him.

By this time, Mum and Dad were too fond of little Ralph to let him go. He was spoilt rotten and knew he could get away with murder. As he got older, he used to stand behind my father and make faces at me. I just wanted to get near him long enough to teach him a lesson.

Chapter Two

Flickers

Australasian Films Studio, Rushcutters Bay, 1923. Bill (second from right) became lab assistant at the studio at the age of fifteen.

THE BEACH AND SPORT were incidental to my life compared to my love of the pictures. The movies provided the opportunity to look into other lives. I got to know all the movie houses around me. But it was at the open-air flickers at Hampden Oval, the place where my imagination had been sparked when I was five, that I learned how the film appeared on the screen.

The operator hand-cranked the Biograph machine on the back of a truck. A lamp illuminated the film, and if it was not turned at the correct speed of sixteen images a second, or sixty feet of film, it could burst into flames. It was a dangerous job for the operator, who also had to keep the light at the right level. Films became known as flickers, because the image flickered as the film was projected onto the screen.

Further up Cascade Street in Paddington, an enterprising bloke named Moodie began another open-air theatre in a rock quarry. As it was below street level, kids and anyone else who did not want to pay could stand on tiptoes, peer over the fence and watch the show for free. The films were silent, so we knew what was going on by reading the titles. Before long, Moodie struck the same problem as the Hampden Oval proprietor – when it rained, patrons sat ankle-deep in water.

Despite the setbacks, Sydneysiders loved the pictures. City picture theatres drew full houses, and you had to book tickets for all cinemas on Saturday nights. In the eastern suburbs around Paddington, there were three picture theatres within a mile of each other. The best was on Oxford Street, Paddington. Here, the audience was completely protected from the weather. If you went to the theatre on Jersey Road, Woollahra, you could sit under cover on three sides but the centre seats were under the stars. The music pit, where a pianist, a violinist and a cornet player sat, was also sheltered. When it rained, we ran to the sides to continue watching the show under the cover.

When I was seven, my parents took me to a show at the Woollahra Theatre. During interval a singer belted out a song on the open-air stage. By second verse it had started pouring with rain, but he stayed on stage and kept singing, even though the crowd in the centre seats had already scurried to the sides for cover. He certainly earned his quid that night. That theatre eventually closed to become a lumberyard.

The third theatre, a tin shed at Five Ways, Paddington, stayed open until the introduction of sound. I joined the stampede of kids running to the Saturday matinees. As the lights dimmed and the show began, the roar of excited children sounded like a low-flying aeroplane. When the picture hit the screen, the noise ceased, as though the engine had shut down. It was my regular haunt because it showed comedies and serials, starring Charlie Chaplin, Australia's Snub Pollard and Fatty Arbuckle. Charlie Chaplin had to be the greatest comedian of all time. We screamed with laughter at his shows. In *The Rink* (1916), he showed his skill on skates, while in *Easy Street* (1917) he portrayed a policeman, and in *The Cure* he gave a memorable performance as an alcoholic who goes to a mineral springs hotel to be cured. A favourite of mine was *The Perils of Pauline* (1914) a twenty-part serial starring Pearl White. Each episode would end with Pearl in dire trouble. We were urged to 'see what happens to Pearl next Saturday', as we watched her helplessly tied to the train tracks, an old puffer bearing down on her. Houdini, another favourite, never failed to excite the kids. Would he escape after being locked in a trunk and thrown into the harbour? No matter how many chains and padlocks were used, Houdini reappeared every week.

A piano provided sound for the flickers. The pianist watched the screen carefully for a change of mood: high-speed music accompanied chases, love scenes needed a dreamy score, whereas fight scenes required heavy music, and deaths or hospital scenes something sad and melodramatic.

Flickers of History

My first experience of a big Hollywood movie was a racing story called *The Whip*. My parents took my sister Kathleen and me to the Fiveways flea-house in 1917. There, aged nine, I fell in love with the blonde heroine. There was a horse race, of course, with the villains trying to dope the favourite, but the hero, together with his beautiful accomplice, fought off the baddies and lived happily ever after. That year, my sister and I were allowed to go to the Saturday matinees by ourselves.

We usually chose the Westerns, starring people like Tom Mix, Harry Carey, Will Rogers, William S. Hart and William Farnum. Farnum was a fantastic actor, whom I later saw on broadway in New York. The best thing about him, I discovered, was his voice . . . yet he was a star of the silent movies! One of his co-stars was a stunning blonde Australian, Louise Lovely – once known as Louise Carbasse – who went to Hollywood as a teenager, where she achieved great success.

I could not help but be affected by this new world, often wagging school just to see a new film. I was addicted.

Apart from the flickers, dancing and girls were my main teenage pursuits. In the early years, there were dances for kids at the town hall, but, by fifteen, I clamoured to get into the dance halls up to four nights a week. I grabbed two or three guys and headed out to the dances at the Masonic Hall, the Casino (which was free because Dad knew the doorman) or the Palais, which was managed by an American who surrounded himself with a team of bouncers to keep order. There was usually some form of entertainment at the dance, such as the professional couples who gave enthusiastic demonstrations of the latest dance steps from Europe. Lina Watson and Syd Halliday, who later married, were one such couple.

The girls sat in chairs around the walls, while the boys worked up the courage to ask them to dance. If you started walking towards an intended partner, it was usually pretty easy to tell if she would accept or decline. If keen, she watched as you came towards her, but if uninterested she turned away and pretended not to notice you. If you foresaw a rejection, you could save pride by veering off in another direction.

Some of the boys drank quite a bit at the dances. I never drank much, mainly because I could not afford it. There were quite a few fights between various 'pushes' or gangs – particularly at Bondi, then a pretty rough suburb – where the boys used to fight each other by hurling blue metal. There were two cops at the time walking the Bondi beat: one nicknamed Hands Up, who broke up many fights as he did his rounds; and the other known as the Mad Digger because he had just returned from the war. Hands Up got his nickname from his practice of waving his arms as he moved in to arrest someone. The Mad Digger's method was more forthright – he threw a punch and asked questions later. We had a run in with the Digger in the foyer of the Sixways movie house in Bondi. The Mad Digger walked in and punched my friend in the stomach, leaving him doubled over with pain. I shouted to my mother, who rushed out of the theatre and abused the cop. The Digger, all puffed up, with his thumbs resting in his cape, asked to talk to her outside. I yelled, 'don't go, Mum,' and luckily she refused. Dad took us to make a complaint at the Hunter Street

Flickers of History

police headquarters, where we were all questioned. Three weeks later the matter was dropped, and the Mad Digger was quietly transferred to the country.

At fifteen, I told my father that it was time I got a job. Of course, the job I wanted was in the film business, but I did not know how to go about getting into the trade. We got in touch with Walter Sully, the chain-smoker who saved his cigarette cards for me ten years earlier. Sully was chief newsreel cameraman at Spencer's Studio, which had been taken over by Greater Union–Australasian Film Studios. Each week it produced the silent *Australasian Gazette*, the second oldest newsreel in the world. Sully sprang to mind because he had recently been photographed skating around the top of the Commonwealth Bank building in Martin Place, the tallest building in Sydney at the time. The crazy guy had skated around the three-foot wide ledge, seven floors up, making the front page of the newspapers for his troubles.

When my father rang him, Walter was as accommodating as he had been with his cigarette cards. I began as a messenger boy, sweeping floors, burning waste film, locking up every night, and delivering all the messages by tram to the bosses at head office. The managing director, Stuart F. Doyle, was a real showman. Back then, he was called flamboyant; now he would be called an entrepreneur. My other job was to deliver the prints of the newsreels every Saturday morning to the film house for screening. It was a pretty basic job, but I was mad about it. I received fifteen shillings a week, but five days a week was not enough. I worked on my weekends, going out with Walter and Bill Trerise as a camera assistant, which meant I carried the tripod. On the weekends, the crew got one shilling and sixpence, about enough for lunch. Every Saturday and Sunday it was the same – a Sergeant's pie, a buttered roll and a pot of tea, with table service, but no tips. No one has ever made a meat pie to rival Sergeant's.

Under the tutelage of the lab superintendent, Charlie Ellis, I learned how to develop movie film on a rack and tanks, make up the chemicals for developing negative and positive, and print the negative onto the positive base. Monday morning was always set aside for mixing chemicals. The chemicals were measured, weighed and dropped into a wooden tank that took thirty gallons, with water added by a hose. As the temperature changed outside, the temperature of the chemicals had to be regulated by adding ice or hot water. As the solution became weaker towards the end of the week, negatives took longer to develop.

Negatives were developed on wooden racks that took two hundred feet of film. The racks were dropped into the developing tank and the film agitated to ensure no bubbles formed. The tank took four racks of two hundred feet of film and after three or four minutes the operator would check to see if the image was coming through. The racks were agitated until he considered them ready. After being washed and fixed to clear all chemicals, the film would get a final rinse, after which it was dried and wound onto a drum that held one thousand feet. Negatives were then edited and printed onto a colour base to suit the story and the processed rolls spliced together into one-thousand foot reels for screening. The job at Australasian Films required knowledge of all fields rather than an area of specialty, and I benefited from that policy.

As all the films were silent, the studio hired two famous artists, Bill Cathcart and Harry Dale, to print the title cards by hand using a brush and ink. The cards were photographed to link the scenes together to tell the story. Without those title cards, it would have been impossible to understand what was going on.

The studio produced three famous cameramen: Walter Sully, Bill Trerise, and Lacey Percival. There were also freelance cameramen, such as the Higgins brothers (Ernie, Tas and Arthur), Bill Jackson and Francis Birtles. They were pioneers of motion pictures, responsible for many early Australian productions. Jackson and Birtles roamed Australia to shoot what were known as 'scenics', to screen in the first half of the program.

One of my favourite places in the studio was the vault where they stored films that had finished their run in the theatre. There I found the films of my youth – the shows starring Charlie Chaplin, Snub Pollard, John Bunny and Fatty Arbuckle. It was a veritable Aladdin's cave of treasures for a film-mad boy. I would run my hand over the dusty canisters containing the shows that I had spent so much time and money watching. The magic of those early movies was still there, ten years after I had first seen them, and it would remain for the rest of my life.

The vault contained some of the first Australian productions, including *The Story of the Kelly Gang*, made in 1906, and *Eureka Stockade* and *Robbery Under Arms*, both released in 1907. *For the*

Term of his Natural Life, based on the novel by the Australian author Marcus Clarke, was a great story that has been filmed several times. The studio produced a remake in 1927 directed by Norman Dawn, a former Hollywood cameraman turned director. It was, at the time, the most expensive picture ever made in Australia, with a price tag of £60 000. Eva Novak, a beautiful blonde star famous for Hollywood Westerns and action pictures, starred opposite George Fisher, a New York stage actor. During the shoot, Fisher hired two big lugs to act as bodyguards, and, when filming took place in Sydney, he stayed across the road from the Bondi Hotel. Dunstan Webb, Arthur Tauchert and Arthur McLaglen played the villains. McLaglen, a boxer and vaudeville performer, had a brother, Victor, who later won a Best Actor Oscar for his role in *The Informer* (1915).

Dawn was the first director to introduce a range of trick shots to the Australian film industry, including the split frame, where four images are split in the one frame. I revered this man, who was also a great camera mechanic – but then I was in awe of anyone who had come out of Hollywood.

The directors used megaphones to yell to the actors, and usually made their displeasure with performances perfectly clear. Some Hollywood directors showed their fury by hurling their megaphones at the actors.

Like all companies, Australasian Films had its fair share of nepotism. Dawn brought Paramount News' chief cameraman, Len Roos, from Hollywood to shoot the film. The studio manager, Frank Marden, had appointed a mate from Melbourne, Bert Cross, as the number two cameraman. But Roos made it clear he wanted Trerise as his number two. With a knowledge of the movie camera second only to Sully's, it should have been Trerise's job. At the end of the day, the management backed Cross but Roos, who was in the studio and away from management, retained Trerise as his number two. Although my role was minor – I was called on to shoot the crowd scenes and print the film – it was an extremely proud moment to see the film screened. It remains, in my opinion, one of the best technically produced and acted films of the silent era.

In its opening week, *The Term* took £10 000 at Union Theatres' Crystal Palace in George Street, Sydney, where it ran for a record eleven weeks. The top price at the time for a seat was ten shillings. Dawn followed *The Term* with *The Adorable Outcast* (1928), starring the American actress Rene Adore. His two projects were the last big films made for the silent screen.

Beaumont Smith, whose films include *The Hayseeds* (1933) and *Splendid Fellows* (1934), was one of the busiest directors in the studio. Together with his brother Eric, who was a film editor, Beau produced and wrote his own scripts. One of his leading ladies was Lotus Thompson, a local girl from Coogee in Sydney, who was striking and photogenic. Lotus left for Hollywood in 1924 and after making a few movies, married and settled in America.

Beaumont made the 'cheapies', which meant he didn't pay the extras. He just rounded up the locals from the suburbs surrounding the set and asked them if they would like to be in a movie. Most people jumped at the chance, even though they weren't paid a cent. They were provided with lunch, which consisted of a pie, a buttered roll, a pot of tea, and, if they were really lucky, a slice of current cake. The extras didn't mind one bit. They were on the big screen, even if only for a fleeting moment. At least they would have something to tell their friends.

Raymond Longford was another of the studio's great directors. He was responsible for the screen adaptation of C.J. Dennis' *The Sentimental Bloke* (1919), starring Arthur Tauchert and Lottie Lyell. When the film opened in the Hoyts Theatre in George Street, Sydney, on 18 October 1919, Tauchert spoke to the audience before the show. He was the quintessential Australian larrikin – a real character. I first met Tauchert, who was a friend of my father's, when he did our make-up for the school plays at the Paddington Town Hall. He was funny and entertaining – but also tough. He belonged to a gang, known as a 'push'. Every suburb had its push, and when they got together it normally ended in a brawl. The big night for the push was Friday night, a shopping night in all capital cities. The shops were open until 9 pm, attracting crowds of mostly well-dressed people, who were just as keen to watch as to shop. It was a great chance for young blokes to eye the girls.

One particular Friday night, Tauchert's push was in town when they came up against the Balmain push in the middle of Sydney's Pitt Street. A brawl broke out, with Tauchert in the thick of it, but when the paddy wagons came to drag off the protagonists, Tauchert played his best role yet. As his mates were being dragged into the waiting paddy wagons, Tauchert cried out, 'a lot of larrikins attacked me.' His convincing performance saved him from being arrested.

At that stage, I thought little about the rest of the world, with the exception of Hollywood. Australia was so isolated from the western world; it took six weeks to get here by ship from Europe, and three weeks from America. Those destinations were just names to most people, as only rich people travelled overseas.

Occasionally, overseas came to us. The vaudeville shows at the Tivoli Theatre attracted international stage artists. The shows turned over every two or three weeks with all sorts of acts, including juggling, athletic contortionists and tap dancing. One of the most memorable was, strangely enough, a champion swimmer named Annette Kellerman, who appeared on stage in a tight-fitting, red rubber suit, sending all the young men in the audience into paroxysms. Kellerman, no stranger to daring swimming costumes, found herself arrested in the US in 1910 for indecent exposure. Although she had a rather plain face, Annette had a magnificent body that was accentuated by all that red rubber. She performed one act in a six-foot-high glass tank full to the brim with water. She explained her act to the goggle-eyed audience before diving. Most of her act was spent beneath the surface, performing underwater ballet which, I guess, was the forerunner to synchronised swimming. Apart from being a champion swimmer and Vaudeville star, Kellerman went on to appear in several films and to write several books. Her life story was told in 1951 in the film *The Million Dollar Mermaid*.

Chapter Three

America

Filming the sign-up for a middleweight boxing contest between Richards and Sabatino, November 1938.

BY NINETEEN, I was beginning to grow impatient. I had learned much in the past five years in the film studio. The staff had grown from nine to thirty, and we had all been moved to a larger studio in Bondi Junction. I felt confident in my job – confident enough to leave for Hollywood.

The ship was called the *Niagara* and my parents saved the fare to pay for a third-class passage to Vancouver, Canada. From the moment I boarded the *Niagara*, I realised I was wet behind the ears, and it was not because of the sea. As soon as the ship got outside the Heads, the seasickness hit and I vomited for four days straight. On top of that, I got terribly homesick, though I was barely a week away. Travelling was not how I had imagined it. I shared a poky cabin with three other men, who were all older and wiser. One was a pianist – a huge bloke – who fell in love with a woman on board.

Once faced with a new country, my torment ended – there were new lives on which to focus. On arriving in Vancouver, I noticed the most minute details of the place – all the small things that made it different from Australia. I marvelled at the shops that sold nothing but buttermilk. And the pineapple and orange bars that served up freezing cold glasses of juice.

As I wandered around town, I saw posters for the Ringling Bros. Circus. As kids, we would look forward to the circus every year at the old hippodrome near Central Station in Sydney. I knew my Aunt Ivy worked for May Wirth, a top equestrian with Ringling Bros. and Barnum & Bailey Circus. Ivy had worked for May's relatives, Mr and Mrs George Wirth, who, along with George's older brother Philip, owned the largest and most successful circus in Australia. They had a massive house in Rushcutters Bay, where Ivy worked as a housekeeper and companion for Mrs Wirth. The Wirths took Ivy around the world with them, and the three of them stayed with May while they were in America. May was so impressed with the way Ivy looked after her employers that she offered her a job, but Ivy declined. The party travelled to London before arriving back in Australia, and the Wirths presented Ivy with a fur coat in appreciation for all her work. (They had previously given her a diamond and opal broach.) But Ivy thought she would do better in America, and, soon after their return, announced she was leaving to work for May. I never understood why she left the Wirths, but it showed her true character and lack of gratitude.

The Australian-born May was a star of the sawdust ring with the highlight of her act being a backward somersault on the back of a galloping horse. She had travelled to America with her husband Frank in 1913 and walked into a job at the Ringling Bros. Circus, where she joined Con Colleano and Lillian Leitzel as the major attractions in the Big Top. Ringlings boasted 'The Greatest Show on Earth'. It was certainly true – they beat Wirth's Circus hands down.

I stepped off the boat around the same time as the circus came to town, so by the time I got to the site they were just setting up the huge tent for their two-night stay. As I walked around the site, I saw the general manager chewing out a member of staff. When he had finished, he told the poor employee, 'Never give a sucker an even break.' It appeared to be the philosophy in this competitive new world.

I asked for May, who, after hearing the story of my voyage, immediately invited me to stay at her home with her husband, Frank. Ivy had told her I was coming to America, but I had never expected to stay in her home. Once inside the tent, I noticed a man swinging a golf club. May introduced me but he had obviously already heard my voice. 'I see you have an ocker Aussie with you.' His accent was American, but I soon found out he was as Australian as I. He was Con Colleano. 'What are you doing here?' he asked. I told him I wanted a job in the film business, maybe as a camera assistant.

Con looked fit and slim – a handsome man, who reminded me of Rudolph Valentino. I learned that his mother, a part Aboriginal woman from Narrabri in New South Wales, had married a labourer of Irish ancestry, Cornelius Sullivan, and produced ten children. Con, who was born in Lismore in 1899, was their third. His father, who had spent most of his life working in or running circuses, had taught his children the techniques of the circus and took them through the Australian backblocks with a merry-go-round. It was difficult to make enough money to feed a family of twelve and eventually he sold the merry-go-round. By the time they joined the Rowan Brothers' Circus in 1912, the family changed their name to Colleano. Soon after they headed to Mildura, where they began a new show with the Ashton family. It was a short-lived venture.

Con was only a boy when he began to walk the wire and perform on the trapeze with his older sister, Winifred. He concentrated on his wire act and, with no teacher, he had many accidents trying to perfect his act. The biggest problem was that he could not see his feet when he had completed the forward somersault. No one else had managed to complete this dangerous act on wire.

Con's hard work paid off when he was offered a job at the old Tivoli Circuit in Sydney on a contract worth sixty pounds a week – not bad for 1922. When his contract ended, the Tivoli's main competitor, the Fuller Circuit, won him over. Already he was being hailed as the Wizard of the Wire, a title that stuck. He returned to work for the Tivoli, where he found work for his family. The work got the family back into business, and they toured overseas, with bookings in South

Africa, England and North America. The Colleanos ended up staying in the United States, where they found constant work. As United States immigration laws made it difficult for blacks to find work, Con claimed Spanish heritage.

On his opening night at the Hippodrome, New York's biggest theatre, he had the worst fall of his career. Having nearly completed the forward somersault, he lost sight of the wire, and headed straight for it. Jerking his head to one side, he took the full force of the steel with his chest. It caused excruciating pain, but he tried two more times. Each time, he missed. Determined to complete the act, he asked the manager to turn off the footlights. Without the blinding light from the floor below, Con sailed through the act, drawing applause that seemed to go on for hours. A ten-day hospital stay brought him back down to earth. He returned to the Hippodrome to complete his six-week stint.

Con stayed in the circus business until aged sixty, and, in 1966, he was inducted into the American Circus Hall of Fame in Sarasota, Florida. May Wirth and Con's older sister, Winnie, were also honoured.

That first night in Vancouver, I was treated to The Greatest Show on Earth, sitting in one of the best seats in the house. It was far more sophisticated than anything I had seen in Australia, with three rings and two stages, all performing at once. With so much happening, I found it hard to concentrate on one particular act. However, when any one of the three stars performed, other action stopped and the lights dimmed, so that all eyes were directed to one stage. The ringmaster introduced each act and gave a running commentary for the stars. Con was first up. He missed the wire on his first somersault, but performed the second one perfectly. May completed her backward somersault on the galloping horse with ease. Lillian performed on a cable, attached to the top of the tent. Hanging on with one arm, she completed three hundred revolutions, swinging her whole body over and over again. I could not begin to imagine the strength and stamina required for such an act. The crowd responded with tremendous applause.

After two days, the circus workers packed up in three hours and loaded the tent onto the train for another city. The stars — May, Con and Lillian — had half a train car each as their quarters; May even had a piano in her room. It was a difficult life, travelling all the time, but all those involved seemed to love it. Over winter they all retired to Florida to plan new acts and rehearse old ones.

Before boarding the train for her next engagement, May told me how to find her home in Long Island, New York. I managed to get to Central Station in New York, where a friend of my aunt's met me and put me on the train to Long Island. It was lucky my aunt had taken so much trouble to look after me because I would have been an easy target for a savvy New Yorker on the make — I was so green I reckon I had gum leaves sprouting from my ears.

Forest Hills, one of the elite suburbs of Long Island, was different to anything I had encountered in Australia. The streets were laid out neatly, lined with large trees and perfect houses, which shone with cleanliness. You could smell the affluence. My aunt met me at the station and introduced me to May's husband, Frank — obviously a patient man — who often waited for months to see his wife. Frank had taken his wife's name of Wirth for business purposes. He ran a transport company which looked after the props and baggage for vaudeville acts in New York. It was quite a lucrative business, which allowed him to play golf every afternoon at 4 pm.

I soon discovered it was not going to be easy to get a job in film in America. The unions had the game sewn up, and they certainly weren't going to give this sucker an even break. You had to join the union, stay in the country for two years, and qualify for citizenship before you could apply for a cameraman's job. There were no restrictions on the technical side, so one month after I landed in Forest Hills, I landed a job in the Warner Bros. laboratory, an old Vitagraph studio in Brooklyn. My background helped as my first task involved film checking, a job I had done in Australia, with the only difference being that sound accompanied the films. I learned how to print film the American way and to repair torn negatives, a handy skill to have in a film laboratory.

By 1927 Warners Theatre on Broadway was the only theatre in New York that had been wired for sound. It was a bold experiment for a studio in the process of going broke. They secured the famous stage and radio singer Al Jolson to star in the first 'talking' picture, *The Jazz Singer*, which premiered on 6 October 1927. Jolson, the son of a rabbi, was a singer with a difference, who smeared his face black to appear on stage. In *The Jazz Singer*, the sound was recorded onto discs before being matched to the image. Warner Bros. had to rely on the theatre operator to kick off the picture on cue with the disk. It was, of course, a disaster in some theatres. If an operator was off cue, the movie had to be started all over again. Other studios scoffed at the notion of sound, and the press was scathing. Sound would never work, said one short-sighted reviewer, because theatregoers would not be able to talk to one another during the movie.

After Warners ironed out its technical difficulties, it was clear talkies were the way of the future. Technicians around me started working to print the sound on the side of the image, so that it could never get out of sync. It would require a change from sixteen feet of film per minute to twenty-four feet per minute and the replacement of every Biograph machine in the country. Although other studios perfected this process first, the innovation of sound put Warners back in the black. It was actually Fox Films that produced the first full feature in colour with sound incorporated.

There were over three hundred staff at the Warner lab and, although I took a lot of ribbing because of my accent, they were great people to work with. I became aware that words like 'may' sound like 'my' in an Australian accent. When I said 'g'day', it sounded like 'g'die'. Because of this, I decided to speak 'American', and eventually I passed myself off as one of them. Even today, people still ask about my American accent.

When I got the job, I left Forest Hills where I had stayed for one month, and found my own accommodation. I got an attic room with a Jewish family who had a house in Brooklyn. They had all sorts of rules and regulations, particularly about girls, but that didn't bother me because I couldn't afford to keep a girl anyway. It was a spartan existence. I had a little gas ring in my room so I could make a cup of hot chocolate or burn some toast, but most of the time I just ate out. Every morning I bought breakfast at a delicatessen that served short-order meals, like ham and eggs, for a quarter.

I wasn't there long before Aunt Ivy tired of working for Frank and May. She had a million schemes to get rich and wanted to start her own business. At first I felt sorry for her. My grandfather, Ivy's father, had died when she was four. At fourteen, she was sent out to work to help her mother. She disappeared during the war and came back in 1920 with no money. I never knew where she went, but that's when my mother got her a job working for Mrs Wirth. Ivy had it made at the Wirths – she was popular and a good housekeeper, but had a persistent case of itchy feet. Ivy could never settle down, no matter how good the job.

On the corner of Broadway and Times Square, Ivy set up a soda bar, which was the American version of a milk bar. It sold milkshakes, sodas and ice-creams. I owed her a bit of money and was keen to repay her for her kindness to me at the Wirths', so I agreed to work there at nights. At the end of three months, knew the trade pretty well.

Every day at 5 pm, I swapped my lab coat for a soda jerk's uniform. Dressed in a white cap, a white shirt and an apron, I mixed what I considered the most delicious milkshakes in town, by first smearing the inside of a tall glass with fresh whipped cream then pouring in the milkshake. I would slide the glasses down the counter top to the waiting customer, never spilling a drop.

Flickers of History

The soda bar was next to a theatre, which provided a steady stream of customers. Over those three months, I ran into George Fisher, the lead from *For The Term of his Natural Life*, and an Australian musician who played the theme music for the pictures. I could never remember her name, but she had come to New York to join her boyfriend. She was a pretty girl but seemed wary of me. I guess she did not want to give people the wrong idea.

Just as everything was going smoothly, Ivy got sick of the soda bar. She took a couple of rooms in the New York Times building while she considered her next venture. I went to live with her to keep her company. It was the noisiest spot you could find, with trucks rumbling out at 1 am to deliver the day's news. Surprisingly, I did get used to it, but, before long, I was told we were moving again.

This time, Ivy took out a whole floor of a building on 47th Street, near Broadway. We had two of the nine rooms and the rest were rented out – sometimes by the hour. Ivy wasn't fussy. A homosexual couple, who used to fight like Kilkenny cats, shared one room. They were nice enough to us and never tried anything on me. One night they had a serious fight, and punches were thrown. One bloke stood at the top of the stairs and threw a whole dinner set down on the other guy, cutting his hand quite badly.

This way of life came as a total surprise to me. Before I went to America, I thought I had seen a lot, but my time with Ivy showed me that I was a babe in the woods. Nothing surprised Ivy. For me, it was a real eye-opener. One night, two Jewish boys, one of whom had got me the job at Warner Bros. invited me to a homosexual ball. I figured it wouldn't hurt to have a look from the gallery. Everyone was dressed like women, with make-up, dresses – the works. You would have sworn they were all women, dancing together.

Usually the police were on hand in case some troublemakers turned up to punch up a few homosexuals. That night, however, the police came to raid the joint. These were the days of Prohibition, but most of the guys had a hipflask tucked into their dresses. Quick as a flash, all the flasks were thrown onto the floor. No one could or would tell the police who owned the flasks, which were by now strewn across the dance floor. The police solved the problem by arresting the organisers, leaving everyone else free to go.

A restaurant was Ivy's next venture. She set it up next to a theatre which had a five-hour show in progress, so patrons would come in at the 7 pm dinner break. Ever loyal, I worked as a waiter. Some nights were better than others and, although she did make a bit of money, the standards were never very high. I became convinced Ivy was not going to make it in the restaurant trade when we ran out of food one night. The chef ordered me to save the food that came back on the plates. If a potato came back, it was slipped onto the next plate and sent back out. A lot of people got second-hand food that night.

To no one's surprise, the restaurant didn't last long. When Ivy took another floor of rooms, I announced that if her latest venture failed I would not move with her again.

After eighteen months at Warner Bros., I moved to the editing rooms at Fox Films laboratory in New York. Outside working hours, I had still mixed with an interesting crowd from Warners.

Flickers of History

We spent a lot of time going on picnics on the Hudson River. Life in New York differed from anything I had experienced in Sydney. Married women worked in America, something I had never seen in Sydney. Relationships seemed open – many couples I knew were separated, and affairs raged between the workers, whether they were single, married or divorced. All of this was totally foreign to my very Catholic upbringing.

Arriving, as I did, in the middle of prohibition, the whole of New York seemed consumed with the search for a drink. I wasn't much of a drinker, but all my friends were pretty keen on the stuff. My first invitation to a Warners party came with instructions to pick up the illegal gin from a den in the middle of Harlem, the black area of Manhattan. They figured the police would never suspect someone who looked as green as me.

All the way up on the train, I wrestled with my conscience. What if I got caught with alcohol? Could I go to jail in America? Would they confiscate my passport? I found the Harlem distillery – a bathtub in a run-down house, operated by two big black guys. I bought two bottles of gin, which I carried in plain paper bags under my arms through the streets of Manhattan. On the train ride back to the party, I was so convinced everybody on the train was staring at me that sweat trickled down my neck. With guilt written all over my face, I expected a tap on the shoulder by a policeman at any time.

When I got to the party, a large glass punchbowl full of orange juice and ice sat in readiness. All it needed was the gin. A couple of glasses and the guests were off. Guys chased girls. Girls chased guys. I was stunned. Being sober probably made things appear far worse.

If New Yorkers couldn't find a private party where they could have a drink, there was always a speak-easy. These sly grog joints were usually found in back alleys or dark corridors. For a quarter, I would buy a glass of 'near beer'. The food was free because it encouraged patrons to come in for a drink. Occasionally, the cops raided the speak-easy. They rolled the kegs onto the streets and spiked them, leaving the thirsty patrons to watch as the gutters ran amber with their favourite drink.

After filling up with grog at the speak-easy or watching the theatre, many customers went on to the flea circus, where they could see freakish acts for next to nothing. My Australian mate, John Dobbie, spruiked at a flea circus on 42nd Street. The free acts included the Fighting Fat Sisters, two obese women who hit each other with boxing gloves, and the Girl in the Glass Bowl, a woman who could eat a banana underwater. For a dime, customers could come up onto the stage to see a striptease by a girl in a box. For openers, Dobbie ran a sword into the side of the box with a great flourish, pretending to cut her in half. To persuade customers, he would reach into the box and pull out an article of clothing, sometimes a bodice or a pair of trousers. I helped Dobbie out by acting as the shill, playing the eager customer by running up the stairs at every new show. Just like sheep, the rest of the curious patrons would follow.

But the star attractions were the Half-Man-Half-Woman and the flea circus. The Half-Man-Half-Woman, who claimed to be born in Sydney, was supposedly male on one side and female on the other, and dressed accordingly. You could see the hairy arms and legs and flat chested on the male side, and the smooth arms and legs and what appeared to be a breast on the other side. No one knew exactly what lay underneath, but customers paid a quarter just to see it.

The main act was a flea circus in which real fleas, held with fine chain leashes, were trained to perform for audiences, who obviously required top eyesight. The trainer fed the fleas with his own blood from his arm, and spurred them on to kick cotton balls and pull tiny little wagons. It was a bizarre act. I figured if you could train fleas, you could train anything.

I spent most of my nights at the flea circus with Dobbie or with my friends from Warners. As the hub of New York nightlife, 42nd Street was the place to be.

All the time, the tension was building with Ivy. I was getting ready to go out one night, when an argument broke out. As I shined myself up, greasing my hair back, Ivy complained that I should stay home and keep her company. Staying home was the last thing on my mind, particularly given the situation. Ivy lost her temper and hurled the contents of a sugar bowl at my head, raining sugar all over me. It stuck to my hair like sprinkles on an ice-cream cone. That was it, I moved out.

All the elements of my life in New York pointed to a change of scenery. My American visa was coming to an end, and I had to leave the country to renew it. I decided it was time to leave town.

Months earlier, I had stayed with the Demers, a large French Catholic family in Montreal I had met through one of Ivy's friends. The Demers had taken a shine to me and spoiled me during my three-day trip. When I left, they extended an invitation for me to come to Montreal to live, which I had declined because of my job at Fox. Now their offer looked tempting. I didn't want to go back to Australia yet, and, as the Depression was hitting America, my restricted passport would make it impossible to stay and work.

Albert Demers worked on the Canadian National Railway, and his wife, Beatrice, raised their eleven children with an iron fist. She ran the whole house, including her husband, and we all knew when she said 'no' it meant just that. They made me feel like one of the family, even though I really was a complete stranger. Dinner time was the most entertaining time in the Demers' home. My French was appalling, so those children who could speak English would explain the details of the exchanges.

Christmas Day and New Year's Eve were great celebrations with the Demers. The table was laid with all sorts of goodies before we all went off to mass. Alfred made his own wine from beetroot, a delicious drop that kept any party going all night. The main meal was at lunchtime on Christmas Day, which included a huge turkey served with freshly cooked cranberries. The Montreal beer flowed. After home life with Aunt Ivy, it was heaven.

When I began the search for a job, Beatrice gave me some advice. 'Beel,' she said, 'why don't you pay a visit to Mount Royal Cathedral. Say the rosary while walking on your knees to the front entrance, and your prayers may be answered.'

The cathedral was built on the top of a small mountain in the heart of Montreal. The idea was to shuffle on your knees up the hill to the front, praying as you went. I did this and finished my prayers off inside the cathedral. There, hanging from the ceiling, were the crutches of all the crippled people who had been healed.

Flickers of History

My prayers were answered and I got a job. There was only one film laboratory in Montreal, so I had no hope there in the middle of the Depression. Only the lucky ones had work in those days, so I felt extremely blessed when I landed a job as a theatre usher at the Palace Theatre.

Sound had became an important asset to a film, almost to the point where the picture quality did not matter as much as the sound. In collaboration with Western Electric, the theatre companies came up with an idea of installing a control box in every theatre that had sound. Ushers had to be checked for their hearing and their ability to operate the sound box. After ushering people into the theatre, my job was to decide how loud the sound should be to ensure it could be heard in every corner of the movie houses. I phoned through to the film operator to let him know whether to increase or lower the volume. This system operated for about two years before sound was regulated. Today, it feels like sound is only geared for one level – LOUD.

After five years in America and Canada, it was time to come home. I was sad to leave the Demers, but excited at the prospect of seeing my parents again. By chance, I travelled home on the *Niagara*, the boat that had taken me to Vancouver. (It was later sunk during the war.) In November 1931, I rejoined the old studio, which was to be renamed Cinesound Production in 1932. It had just produced its first newsreel in sound, called the *Cinesound Review*. My old mentor, Walter Sully, was the chief cameraman. Stuart Doyle, who had become managing director of the new company, had appointed Ken Hall as the general manager of the studios. Hall assumed responsibility for the production of the company's first sound features, *On Our Selection* (1932). The film starred an old stage actor, Bert Bailey, in the lead.

The small silent film studio, which had been built in the centre of a skating rink at Bondi Junction, needed to be made soundproof. (The building was still used each night for skating.) The ingenuity of the crew meant Greater Union could escape without an expensive renovation. It was simply lined with egg cartons. The cameraman had to sit in an airtight box and shoot the film through a glass window. The cameraman had to come out every ten minutes to get fresh air, both into his lungs and into the box. At that stage, I was in charge of the dark room and because of my experience with sound in America I was able to introduce a few techniques. In time, I moved into the editing room and became newsreel film editor, before joining Associated Press as a photographer and contact man.

Nothing much had changed in Australia, so I soon fell into the same circle of friends around the eastern suburbs, and it didn't take me long to get into the swing of the weekly dances. Although many of the dance halls had closed down, it was still the thing to do. I had no intention of tying myself down, and so I met lots of girls, some of whom would come home for supper on a Sunday night. My parents had a way of letting it be known whom they liked and whom they considered inappropriate.

St Anne's was our local church, built on an old sand hill that became an intersection called Seven Ways. As a boy, I used to slide down the sand hill with my friends and pretend we were trapped in the Sahara desert, chasing each other until we got to the beach and into the surf.

I had been back in Australia for two years when I saw a girl at Sunday mass. I noticed her hat first, a dainty hat on a dark-haired beauty. 'What am I doing wasting my time with other girls?' I thought.

At a dance soon afterwards, I spied the brunette across the room with another man. The dance involved the men going one way and the women another, allowing you to change partners regularly. She was coming my way, but it looked as though I wasn't going to reach her. When the time came, I lunged at the poor girl to find out her name. Mary Margaret Murphy – a milliner, which explained the cute hat.

The next time I went to mass, I waited behind and followed Mary out the door. Running to catch up with her, I offered to walk her home. I found out later that she had already told her mother about me, and how I had met her a number of times. Her family was not terribly impressed with me because of my black and white shoes, which were the height of fashion in the US but had not been seen in Bondi in 1933. I managed to get her away from the family for a walk along the beach.

For our first date, I suggested a movie at the State Theatre in the city centre. Being a Greater Union movie house, of course, I could get in for free. It was all going well, so I asked her to come back for dinner at my parents' house. At last, I brought home someone they liked, and I liked her too. My parents had met a number of girls but, after Mary left, they told me, 'We like the Irish girl.'

Mary had clicked with my mother, who was confined to bed most of the time by then with an illness later diagnosed as cancer. Mary spent quite a lot of time with her after the diagnosis. Her visits gave Mum enough time to give Mary a detailed inventory of my faults, my bad temper, and the fact I was spoiled rotten. She was more help to my mother than my sister because Kathleen would get very upset every time she saw Mum. Kathleen got married in the final weeks of Mum's life; my mother was in so much pain she had to be carried into the wedding.

Mum died at the age of forty-six from breast cancer. After she had surgery to remove one breast, she was fine for about a month before she developed a pain in her knee. Doctors could not diagnose the problem, but the cancer was obviously spreading. She was left with only pain-killers and prayer.

Her death affected us all differently. It spurred Mary and me into action, and we got married within a month of her death. My father was devastated. He broke up the house after she died, giving away most of their possessions. He took Ralph and moved into a boarding house, and later they moved in with Kathleen. Dad never got over Mum's death.

After the capture of the 'Pimple' on the peak of Shaggy Ridge, it was discovered that eight Japanese soldiers had held the Australians at bay for several weeks.

A newsreel theatrette in Pitt Street, Sydney, showing the documentary Jungle Patrol *on its first screening in 1944.*

Part II

War

A picture from Jungle Patrol. *Biscuit Bombers are here shown flying over New Guinea.*

Eichelberger, Blamey and Carty after covering the Buna campaign. Photograph: Cliff Bottomley.

Chapter Four

Call-up

Bill Carty with his wife and three children on Bill's last night before leaving for the war in 1942. He next saw them ten months later on a fortnight's leave.

WHEN I RECEIVED THE CALL-UP in 1941, our children, Helen and Jim, were toddlers, and Mary was pregnant with our third child, Pauline. I was shocked, and Mary was worried about how she would cope by herself with three young children. Had I stayed at the film studio, I would have been protected because we processed all the film for the Department of Information (DOI). The notice instructed me to attend a medical examination at Waverley Park in Sydney. It suggested I bring two sandwiches, a razor and some underwear.

I had no great expectations of army life. I had shot a story on the recruitment drives in Martin Place, a large public square in the centre of Sydney. A lot of hairy-chested guys got up to talk about fighting for their country, spurring young men to sign up. Before they knew what hit them, the new recruits were down at the Showground being screamed at by a tough army sergeant. By then, it was too late to back out.

The army had built a small wooden hut at the park for the conscripts in the Bondi–Waverley area. There was a table and a chair, as well as a curtained off area for the doctors to examine the men. I waited until the doctor called my name. It was our old family doctor, Dr Ping, who had performed the operation to remove my mother's breast. I thought he might be sympathetic to my situation and fail me. I reminded him of all my past ailments – a broken thumb, a weak chest from pneumonia, everything I could think of. He passed me one hundred per cent fit.

If I was going to war, it would be as a cameraman. I wanted to record the war on film, so I decided to view conscription as a big break. Dad was a mate of the Minister for Information, Senator William Ashley, so I went down to see him, and, sure enough, the government needed cameramen for DOI, which was in charge of recording the war for Australia. He directed me to a bloke in Martin Place for my instructions on Friday, and, by Monday, I was on the train to Pacific War headquarters in Melbourne.

At my first press conference I met the man with whom I was to have a long association, General Douglas MacArthur, Supreme Commander of the South-West Pacific Area. He had arrived in Australia on 17 March 1942, after escaping from the Philippines with his wife Jean, their son, known as 'little Arthur', and his Chinese amah, Loh Chiu, nicknamed Ah Cheu. MacArthur was a prime target for the enemy. He was forced to leave his home in the dead of night, carrying only a few personal belongings. For his later role in the Philippines, he was awarded the Congressional Medal of Honor.

A month after arriving in Australia, the American general had been made the Supreme Commander of the South-West Pacific Area. MacArthur ran the war from Melbourne, then Brisbane, and later New Guinea and Manila. He began daily briefings for the media, whose stories were sent worldwide. At the first meeting, MacArthur made it clear he wouldn't have any pictures taken. I had no camera with me when the general strode in. He strutted up and down in front of the press corps, reeling off information about the previous day's events. The journalists made frantic and copious notes, but no questions were allowed. About halfway through the conference, a flash bulb went off, stopping the general in full stride. 'Kill that,' he demanded, before continuing with his briefing. The order meant that if any paper used the photograph, their staff would never be allowed to attend future MacArthur briefings.

I languished for months in Melbourne, doing little apart from getting accustomed to the army. On 31 May 1942 three Japanese midget submarines had been discovered in Sydney Harbour, sending the country into a panic. A week later, when the mother submarine fired shells over our house into the Sydney golf course, Mary pushed the children under the dining-room table before diving under there herself. My son Jim told me he was terrified both for himself and his Daddy, who was going off to war. So, like many others, I tried to organise to move my family from Sydney inland to country New South Wales. Such was the fear of invasion, you could have bought any harbourside house for a song. But I could not afford to move them, and they decided to stay on with Mary's mother in Rose Bay.

While I waited for an assignment, I shot a few stories on the troops, including one on the great food provided to the American forces, compared with the basic Australian soldier's diet. Finally, I asked when I would be sent to cover the war. Their reply was to send me to Darwin, with a week in Sydney beforehand to meet Pauline, my seven-day-old daughter.

The Japanese air raids over Darwin had earned the town the label of front line. Over two hundred and fifty people had died in the assault on 19 February 1942. My first assignment in the field marked the beginning of an exciting but apprehensive time. Army public relations had taken over the Parap Hotel, where I stayed with about ten other war correspondents, known as warcos. On every new moon, a wave of eighteen Japanese bombers flew over Darwin between 10 pm and midnight for three nights in a row. A bomb siren warned of their arrivals, and from our foxholes, the warcos watched the planes circle around the town in the moonlight. It was a little tormenting for the cameramen because we could not shoot without sufficient light. All we could do was watch as a film opportunity slipped by.

Due to the predictability of the raids, the Royal Australian Air Force (RAAF) sent up a fighter plane one night in November 1942, flown by a young pilot, Wing Commander Dick Cresswell. As usual, we stood outside our foxholes, watching the bombers. We heard the click of the bombs' release, but we knew we were safe because the bombs always landed forward of the area in Larrakeyah. That night, the squadron leader's plane made a different noise in the sky over us and the chatter of machine-guns signalled the start of a very different raid. I heard the bullets reach their target, and one of the three Japanese bombers at the end of the line burst into flames and split into three sections before falling, as if it were in slow motion. The horizon glowed as the plane hit the ground, about twenty-five miles inland. It was the first and only time a Japanese plane was shot down over Australian territory.

As soon as the sun provided me with enough light to shoot, I headed to the crash site. Nine bodies lay among the wreckage, and a head belonging to one of the crew sat on its stump. It was a gruesome sight, but it stirred no emotion in me. I was disgusted at Japanese aggression in the war, so the deaths of this crew meant nothing to me. I shot the scene and drove back to the RAAF camp to interview the hero.

'I flew up into a black sky,' Cresswell told me. 'In front of me, I could not see a thing – it was just like a black wall. Suddenly, a shadow appeared in front of my plane. I let go with both barrels and scored a hit. I watched the shadow burst into flames and start dropping to the ground.'

I never caught up with Cresswell again after our interview, but I saw eighteen of these air raids before moving on. I heard many years later that he survived the war and lived in Australia. He became the first of many extraordinary people I met during the war years and never heard of again. They remain flickering images in my memory.

Flickers of History

For me, the real war began in New Guinea. I was posted there in 1942 when another DOI cameraman, Frank Bagnall, was brought back to Australia after nearly being killed in Milne Bay. He was in a small boat with *Sydney Morning Herald* photographer, Tommy Fisher, who was below deck, and a crew of natives, when a Japanese plane dropped a bomb. He never saw Tommy or the crew again, and, as the boat began to sink, Frank took off his gear, tied his boots around his neck, and swam for a mile through shark-infested waters to the beach. He found his way through the jungle to natives, who led him back to Port Moresby.

The warcos stayed in a house in Port Moresby when they weren't in the jungle, and I joined the veterans who had already covered the Kokoda Trail and many skirmishes in Europe. Among them was a top newspaper writer, George Johnston, who later wrote a number of novels, including *My Brother Jack*. George had just come back from the front line at Popondetta, on the other side of the Owen Stanley Ranges. He said 'If it's pictures you want, don't lose any time, get over to Popondetta or Buna. The troops are having a torrid time fighting malaria, dengue, as well as the Japanese. The conditions are awful.'

I followed George's advice. The army public relations officer dropped me down at Jackson's airstrip at 5 am and told me to ask one of the 5th US Air Force for a lift to the Australian area in Popondetta. The officer had to request approval for me to enter a war zone, and then I hitched a ride with a couple of flyers, who were dropping off two thousand rounds of twenty-five pounder shells to the Australians. It was my first trip into

Part II: War

a war zone, and there I was, sitting on live shells, flying over the Owen Stanley Range. I realised that, had we been attacked by Japanese planes, we would have been blown out of the sky.

As we began a steep climb to make it over the mountain range, I listened to the conversation between the two pilots, conscious of the cold steel under my trousers. During a quick descent to treetop height on the other side of the range, one said to the other, 'I hope we don't run into that son of a bitch like we did yesterday.' The hair stood up on the back of my neck. If you have ever travelled in an elevator that dropped quickly to the ground floor, you would have some idea of how I felt. My stomach rushed into my mouth as thoughts of dropping planes, enemy fighters and live shells collided. The pilots regularly flew in this way to dodge any Japanese aircraft lurking in the area.

Skimming along the tops of the trees, we flew to Popondetta, but flooding on the airstrip made it impossible to land. We went back to Jackson's airfield, where the pilots checked in and were told to go on to Buna, my second choice. Up in the air again, we made the steep climb and descent over the range before levelling out on the treetops. An airstrip had been cut out of the jungle at Buna by the Americans. I was given strict instructions to jump out of the plane the moment it hit the deck, as it had to be unloaded in a hurry before it was spotted by the Japanese. There was no door on the plane for rapid unloading, so I jumped out with my gear on my back and spotted Australian troops emerging from the jungle. They unloaded the huge shells, before running back, one by one, into the jungle with the fresh ammunition. In two minutes, the emptied plane rolled down the strip for take-off.

I scanned the jungle to get my bearings and find a track to headquarters. The troops had disappeared as soon as the plane was unloaded, so they were no help. There appeared to be a path leading to a clearing that looked like a dumping ground. The Americans used it to store all the gear found in the battlefield. Anything that belonged to the dead or wounded – rifles, canteens, helmets, boots – was brought to this place, and, under the supervision of an American sergeant, was reissued to fresh troops before they headed off into battle. The sergeant gave me directions to the headquarters, seven miles from the airstrip. Considering the hike, I left half my gear with the sergeant and headed off with his warning to 'Keep your eyes peeled for Japanese planes'.

It is difficult to describe the sense of vulnerability, finding yourself alone in a foreign landscape in the middle of a war zone. This was not like any landscape at home. I was used to the narrow streets and terraces of Paddington and Bondi. I had spent a little time in the bush at home, which was far sparser than the jungles of New Guinea, where the kunai grass was six-feet high on either side of the track. Every sound had me immediately scanning the sky for enemy planes. From a distance, the sound of continuous gunfire at the front line mingled with other noises of army life – a combination that inspired a muffled terror in my heart. About halfway along the track, an approaching vehicle sent me diving into the long grass. When I was certain it was two US officers, I jumped back out onto the track as they came close.

No one wore a rank on the front line in case of snipers, so it was impossible to tell whom I was dealing with. The passenger was well over six-feet tall, and the driver was a GI. The tall guy asked me where I was heading. 'To headquarters,' I replied. 'Jump in,' he said, in a slow American drawl. 'I'm just goin' down to the airstrip to pick up one of your generals. He can sit in the front. You're only a little codger, so I'll sit next to you in the back.' With that, he stuck out his hand and said, 'My name is Eichelberger.'

I introduced myself as a cameraman for the Australian government. I discovered when we arrived at the airstrip that no ordinary soldier had been sent to pick up the Australian general. Eichelberger failed to reveal he too was a general. In the next eight years, working with both Australian and American armies, I never heard another general use his surname without a title. Eichelberger stayed a friend throughout the war and the occupation of Japan, and we corresponded until he died in September 1961.

General Edmund Herring, whom we collected from the airfield, was less personable. He was unfriendly and showed no interest when Eichelberger introduced me. I'm sure he would have been more affable if I were a reporter, but a cameraman was of no use to him. We arrived back at headquarters and Eichelberger found a GI to show me where to string up a blanket. The general introduced me to *Life* magazine photographer George Strock, and then entertained us over lunch with stories of his orders from MacArthur: 'He told me when I left Australia, "Bob, I am sending you to Buna. I want you to take it, and don't come back if you don't."' The general wrote about the conversation later in his book, *The Jungle Road to Tokyo*, published in 1950.

Flickers of History

That night, I listened to the hair-raising stories reported by an officer from the front at Buna. The American troops had been sitting in their foxholes for weeks, riddled with malaria and dysentery, waiting to be replaced by Australian soldiers. I asked for permission to go to the front, and Eichelberger arranged for me to travel with a captain the next day.

We set off in the morning, farewelled by the general, to see the Americans, who were fighting on the edge of a plantation. On the way, the captain told me that the general and his two aides toured his front-line troops every day at 4 pm, to talk about the day's fighting and hand out chocolate bars. Eichelberger was nearly shot twice during these tours, but his aides caught the bullets aimed at their boss.

At the end of 1942, the three big fronts were Buna, Sanananda and Gona – the worst battles for the Australians. More Australians were killed in those campaigns than in any other battle in New Guinea. There were pockets of Japanese, Americans and Australians throughout these areas, and overshots from these battles could land anywhere. If you wandered through no-man's-land, you could be killed by a bullet from the gun of any one of these three armies. While we did not know it at the time, the Japanese were on the verge of starvation because their supply lines had been cut.

Lieutenant Colonel Bill Hall, a Victorian, was in charge of the twenty-five pounder guns and troops in the Buna area. Hall, the first Australian I met in the field, quickly filled me in on the army's plans. Australia's 18th Brigade was arriving in a few days and the tanks were about to make their first appearance on the New Guinea battlefields. Brigadier George

Part II: War

Wootten would take charge of all the Australian troops in the area, before an all-out assault on the Buna coconut grove.

Hall took me to their forward spotting post, which was manned by a small band of men from Tasmania. They took it in turns to balance precariously at the top of a fifty-foot tree and report any enemy movements to Hall, who could then direct a barrage of artillery fire. These boys lived around the base of the tree, which was completely surrounded by water. Their boots had rotted away to expose lily white feet that were always wet, the seats had fallen out of their trousers long ago, and their rations were meagre. Blamey's orders were 'shells first, rations second', so most of the time the Australians survived on the generosity of the American troops. They lived on the edge of no-man's-land, yet they were some of the happiest soldiers I ever met. They became part of one of the first newsreel stories I sent back to Australia.

In the first few weeks, I spent quite a bit of time with the spotters, sitting in the fork of that fifty-foot tree, filming Japanese planes. I was on the lookout one day when the sound of planes signalled Japanese bombers, flying at treetop height along the airstrip. At first glance, I thought they were Allied planes but, looking again, the rising sun on the belly of each plane was clear. As I was practically at treetop height, the planes were so close, I could almost make out the colour of the pilot's eyes. With one run of twenty-five feet of film left, I began filming and landed a good shot before running out of film.

Then, in an amazing display, the bellies of the planes opened and dropped coloured parachutes over the Japanese

Flickers of History

lines. It was such a surprise to men used to the green camouflage of wartime. Each parachute carried a large bundle that could easily be seen on the jungle floor. I began shaking with rage, knowing I had shot all my film and the rest of my supply was at the foot of the tree. To climb back down would risk being seen by the bombers, so I put it down to experience.

The spotters had, in the meantime, reported the planes to Lieutenant Colonel Hall using a field phone, and, in ten minutes, three American fighter planes had made several sweeps up and down the strip, strafing and bombing the whole area. I made my way down to the bottom of the tree and, to avoid being hit, joined the spotters in a bizarre dance around the trunk. The Americans had set fire to the kunai grass around us, while totally shooting up the area where the drops had been made. The food supplies must have been in a hell of a mess by the time the Japanese got them. I did manage to get some footage of the Americans, which, along with the Japanese footage, was sent back for the newsreels, but I never saw any of it.

We were still waiting for the Buna push in December 1942 when I celebrated my first wartime Christmas. The American Red Cross brought plane loads of ham, but the Australians brought ammunition, twenty-five pounder shells to be precise, on orders from General Blamey. Luckily for us, the Americans shared their ham with the Australians, who were camped near the American headquarters.

I missed my family terribly, so I was glad of the distraction when Eichelberger invited me to lunch on Christmas Day with seven of his American troops. He had a pretty good set up – a little hut in the middle of the jungle – where he served ham, baked beans and cold grape juice. It was the best lunch I had tasted for a long time.

The Americans were particularly good at catering for their troops all year round. The American Red Cross introduced the first lunch box containing three meals for one soldier – a day's food supply. Later they introduced seven-in-one packages, containing meals for seven soldiers, and then ten-in-one packages. These boxes had everything and they were sumptuous by army food standards. The US troops had canned ham, canned bacon with egg powder, even malted milk powder to mix with their water supplies. Cigarettes and toilet paper were also considered essentials. And these were just the field rations. A kitchen was also set up to serve the men as though they were factory workers. In Buna, two American soldiers worked as cooks just behind the front line, using the food from the ten-in-one packages. The kitchen stayed open all day for shift workers. Soldiers had no trouble finding it – they followed the smell of bacon and coffee. The cooks were never short on customers, and there was a constant flow by their stove.

The Australians, meanwhile, survived on a spartan diet. We were given a few small cans of rations, most containing a meat stew, which we usualy ate cold. We topped up on canned biscuits and fruit, with a few sweets thrown in. It kept us going, but there were definitely no luxuries.

The cooks were quite happy to serve the cameramen filming the American Army, and, in the early days of Buna, I used to drop into the tent quite regularly with another cameraman, Sergeant Syd Woods. We used to joke around, spark off each other, like many Australian blokes. The cooks used to call us Amos and Andy, after two radio comedians who had their own show in America at the time. In return for a few jokes, I was served my favourite dish – corned beef hash.

After dinner, there was nothing else to do but try to sleep. Night-time was when the fear crept in and the Japanese crept out. The jungle was unnaturally silent at night, the war had long since scared the life out of it. Sleep did not come easily to me. I never slept soundly – fear would not allow me to drop into a deeper satisfying slumber. Often we slept in foxholes, which was like being in a burial hole. I would sit – never lie – at one end and doze off occasionally.

One night I heard rustling, like someone crawling through the undergrowth. The rule among the Allies was that you should never leave your spot at night, because of the danger of being killed by one of your own troops, let alone the enemy. It was pitch black and, with a .303 in my hand, I wasn't prepared to take any chances. With my rifle raised, and finger on the trigger, I was ready to shoot. 'Goddammit, where the hell am I?' came the American drawl from somewhere in the night. I was never so glad to hear that accent – an accent that saved his skin.

When we heard barges pulling up on the beach at Buna, we lowered our voices, not knowing which side they belonged to. Out of the darkness came a broad Australian accent: 'Where the hell are we?'

Chapter Five

Action

Bill Carty on his first campaign as war correspondent in Buna, New Guinea. Photograph: Department of Information.

'GUTS AND GAITERS' WOOTTEN made a strong impression on me when he arrived with the 18th Brigade. He had four days to settle in before the planned attack on the coconut grove, and I was required to ask permission for any field trips from the new man in charge. Wootten was a big, rotund man, with an enormous girth and a commanding voice. He felt the heat badly, sweated profusely and always carried a fly-swatter. One warco wrote of the brigadier, 'he was not just another fellow wearing red tabs.' I found his tent, introduced myself, and asked for permission to follow the attack. 'Go wherever you like, but keep your bloody head down,' he shouted. He made it quite clear that I could stay around as long as I liked.

I joined up with a brigade of Australian troops preparing to attack a coconut plantation in Buna. I was facing my first battle with men who had survived the Middle Eastern campaigns. Accustomed to desert fighting, they now had to turn their skills to a war in the tropics, against an unseen enemy. In Buna, I never saw any Japanese attack the Allied troops. The enemy was dug into the coconut grove, in foxholes. When I met our troops behind the lines, they were taking a swim in one of the fresh waterholes that dotted the plantation. They were typical Australians – they liked a bath, for a start – laughing, splashing each other, taking the mickey.

'Wait and see what it will be like tomorrow. We won't be laughing then,' one soldier said to another. How right he was. The Allied forces were preparing to use tanks in the jungle for the first time. The young men relaxing in the waterhole were there to back up the tanks. I had noticed one soldier – a tall, good-looking bloke – having a ball that day in the waterhole. The next day, just fifteen minutes into battle, I saw his body sprawled across a tree trunk, his pack still on his back and his rifle still gripped in his hands. It was one of the many arresting images that remained flickering in my mind after that first day in battle.

We joked publicly, but, privately, we could not ignore the task ahead – no one could predict what would happen. Across enemy lines, the Japanese lay in their foxholes, dug down two levels. They had been pinned down for some time but had survived by making use of the coconut groves. Heavy shelling sent them down to the lowest level, and there they lay, in holes protected by coconut trees. The Japanese positioned cut trees around the holes, as the thick fibre protected them from even the most sustained shelling. Those trees served as the greatest bomb stopper, of all time.

The night was uncomfortable, but the discomfort of the conditions, the heat and the hard ground, was nothing compared to what I felt inside. Would this be my last day? Would I ever see my family again? Dawn broke and, as the troops prepared, I tried not to show how scared I was. The thought crossed my mind that everyone probably felt the same way, but it was no consolation.

The silence of the morning was shattered when we began shelling. At 7 am, twenty-five pounders fired straight into the coconut grove followed by tanks that directed their guns towards the enemy. I must have jumped two feet in the air, for the noise was horrendous. Twenty minutes later it stopped, and the silence was surreal, before a whisper marked the beginning of my first steps from a front line into enemy territory. 'Advance.' The word was passed along the line. The tanks moved off, firing their guns into the jungle as the troops came up behind. Bullets hailed down towards me from an enemy I could not see. I began filming the Australians, who were trying to 'clean out' the foxholes by dropping hand grenades and firing into the darkness. They were having trouble keeping up with the tanks, which had taken off too fast. Even though the action continued around me, I felt like I was alone in the coconut grove.

Flickers of History

We were heading for Cape Endaiadere, on the point of the Buna plantation and the sea. I was in a field of fire, in my first battle, in a strange country, and I had to go to the toilet. If I could have waited, I would have, but this was urgent. 'Wait for me, don't leave me,' I yelled to the nearest troops. I was terrified I would be hit below the belt. It must have been a strange sight – a man with a camera, squatting down in the jungle in the middle of a war.

I ran up to join a machine-gun unit, while, in the distance, tanks scattered throughout the plantation. Some were still shooting, while others were gutted and burning. Those scenes were too remote to make decent pictures. Australian bodies lay on the ground, but there were no enemy bodies to be seen, for they were in their foxholes, dead or alive. I filmed a corporal cleaning out a foxhole with a couple of hand grenades. He wore a sleeveless shirt, bleeding from a wounded arm. When the footage was shown at home, it was written up in a newspaper. A friend kept the article for me. The writer, no doubt some desk-bound scribbler, remarked, 'It was a pity that the troops didn't use real hand grenades.' Hollywood hand grenades burst into flames, lighting up the hero's face for all to see. Real hand grenades are not nearly so dramatic, even though the effects are deadly. All you can see is a small burst of black smoke accompanied by a loud bang. Stand close to a grenade and you never see the broken pieces, but men are killed and wounded.

The unit finally reached Cape Endaiadere, but, before they could set up the machine-guns, we came under heavy fire. I dived behind a coconut tree and lay on my belly on the edge of the beach, next to a soldier. The firing did not let up for two hours. I pressed myself into the sand, willing my body to shrink into the smallest possible target. As we waited, we saw a Japanese soldier in the water about a hundred feet from the beach. His head looked like a coconut, drifting along with the tide. My companion got that head in his sights with his rifle, but, when he began firing, the head disappeared below the surface. After a minute, he rose again, only to duck when the soldier repeated his fire. We could see the shots landing just inches away from him, but none made a hit. Finally, he drifted from view to fight another battle.

The enemy fire died down, and our machine-gun unit was ordered to set up, but not before one of the men took a bullet in the shoulder. It was around 4 pm and I had to make a decision. I could stay with the unit to monitor the action through the night, but there would be no value in taking pictures in the dark. After talking to the lieutenant, I decided to run back to the lines. I was given directions back through the coconut grove, onto the beach and to the command post. I have never run so fast or so far before or since that day.

The night was again uncomfortable, and the coffee in the morning had little effect. I walked up to the front line to meet the men who fought so hard the day before. The casualty tent was full. Soldiers lay clutching their sides, suffering from severe wounds. It was a hell of a shock. The lieutenant, who had advised me to leave the previous night, had a serious gut wound. He was waiting to be treated before shipped back to Port Moresby with a number of his men, who would not see any more action. 'It's lucky you didn't stay,' he told me.

'The Japanese attacked during the night and only half the crew escaped. You would have been either wounded or resting in a hole in the ground.'

There was an emergency operating theatre behind the front lines, where the badly wounded men could be treated before they were sent back to the larger hospital in Port Moresby. Casualty consisted of an open tent held up by four poles with an operating table in the centre. That day, I saw the consequences of the previous day's battle in the coconut grove. A soldier lay on a table, just feeling the effects of an anaesthetic. The doctor was holding his foot, which was barely attached to his leg, there was a gaping hole where his ankle should have been. The doctor told the orderly, 'His leg will have to come off.' Twenty minutes later, the leg had been cut off below the knee and the orderly was holding the stump, dressing it with some kind of mixture. One day in battle, and this soldier would be going home for good.

Most of the tanks had been shot out of action. The tank in which I had ridden was hit – the gunner was killed and the driver lost half his arm when he stopped a shell that had come through the vision hole. The commander of the tank, Jack Latimore, was hit so badly he lost the use of his leg. He spent more than a year in hospital and more time in rehabilitation but pulled through to get married; eventually he could drive and play tennis. In just one day, in just one battle, I could not get over how lucky I was. I vowed I would never return to the front line again. But how quickly I became inured to war. As it turned out, I spent the rest of the war at the front line.

When Buna was captured, the spotters moved further along the airstrip to take up residence in another fifty-foot tree. General Blamey flew in to tour the area with General Eichelberger. The Japanese were still on one side of the strip, so, at one stage, we came under fire, probably from overshooting. Everyone hit the deck, except for Eichelberger, who was the tallest of all of us and nearly sixty to boot. Bob kept apologising to Blamey for getting him into such trouble, but Blamey wasn't much interested — he was on the ground with the rest of us. An American newsreel cameraman had followed me into the ditch. 'I've had it,' he said. 'I'm heading back to the States.' I thought he was joking, but three months later he was back home, writing a book and shooting for the Universal Newsreel.

BRAVE AUSTRALIAN NEWSREEL MEN IN PAPUAN JUNGLE

From George H. Johnston,
"Argus" War Correspondent

SOMEWHERE IN NEW GUINEA
When the battle for Papua finally ends, there will end temporarily one of the most magnificent jobs of work ever done by a handful of young men — the newsreel photographers of the Department of Information.

In recording the battle scenes of one of the most difficult campaigns of the war, the three young photographers who have taken most of the pictures that have thrilled Australians — Damien Parer, of Melbourne; Frank Bagnall, of Sydney; and William

Flickers of History

Carty, of Sydney – have taken almost daily risks in penetrating almost right into the enemy lines. They have worked with battered, second-rate, and often second-hand equipment under conditions in which the best equipment in the world would not be too good.

At the moment Bill Carty is risking his life hourly, day and night, to obtain frontline shots of the Buna fighting. He has been sniped at, bombed, shelled and strafed by Zeros, but he still remains on the job – the only newsreel cameraman forward in New Guinea today. Frank Bagnall is now on the mainland, where his films of the Kokoda track and Milne Bay were shown recently. He lost all his equipment when a small vessel in which he was moving along the north coast was strafed and sunk by Zeros. Bagnall heroically remained on the sinking ship, which was in flames and laden with ammunition, while the Zeros were still strafing, to save the lives of 4 wounded Americans. He then struggled to the shore more than a mile away, with the wounded hanging to a small dinghy.

Damien Parer risked his life for months in the Papuan jungle, obtaining his famous films of jungle warfare and the Kokoda track which America and England hailed as among the greatest newsreel films of the war. To cover the New Guinea campaign, some of the ace newsreel cameramen of the USA were sent here. They had the best equipment that money could buy, but some of them now admit without stint that the Australian newsreel men have beaten them hands down.

Part II: War

DOI had a rule that required any front-line cameraman to return home immediately for two weeks leave after covering a campaign on enemy territory. It was always easy to get a ride back to Australia, as the Americans had planes flying in and out of the country over the Pacific on a daily basis.

For my first home leave, I gave my wife no warning. I turned up on the doorstep at Rose Bay, surprising everyone. The war had totally upset the balance in the family. The older children, Helen and Jim, had missed me because I had previously spent a lot of time with them, but Pauline was only a week old when I left, so I was a stranger to her. My in-laws lived in one half of the house, and we shared the other half. Pauline spent the whole time running to my mother-in-law, which made me feel terrible.

I was there for only a few days of my leave when I came down with malaria. One night in Rose Bay, I woke shivering in a sweat-soaked bed, with a pain in my side from a swollen liver. The doctor sent me to the army hospital in Ryde, where I was treated for three weeks, before being sent to a recovery house. Mary came to visit me every day, carrying a baby on two buses and a train for each trip.

When I recovered, Senator Ashley decided to use me in his campaign to raise money through war bonds. He took me to Tasmania, where I was shown off as a 'fine example' of the men at war. At the same time, I shot a couple of propaganda pieces on companies in Tasmania that were working for the cause, including Cadbury chocolates and Cascade Brewery. I must have drunk too much beer because, shortly after, I was struck down with a relapse of malaria.

Flickers of History

By the capture of Buna in January 1943, I had begun to get a better idea of the difficulties of filming in a war. Apart from vague boundaries to ensure cameramen did not film the same campaigns, we were given no direction on what to shoot or even where to shoot, Film was at a premium and was always in short supply; if you lost your film supply, it could be days before you received new stock. You always thought twice before putting your finger on the trigger. Footage for back home, we sent out by courier through the nearest jungle headquarters. It was marked with handwritten notes, explaining the context, so editors could prepare the story back in Sydney. I had edited some of the early war footage when I was at Cinesound before I was called up, but, once in the field, I had no control over how my footage was used. Editors created the final newsreel, not that it bothered me, for I was too concerned with the day-to-day business of war to worry about how the footage would be cut.

I moved onto Sanananda in January 1943, with Cliff Bottomley, a still photographer for the DOI. We walked the seven miles from Buna to Sanananda with two natives, who carried the gear. It was pouring with rain – one of those tropical downpours to which we had all become accustomed. Brigadier Wootten drove past us in a jeep on his way to take over command of the troops in Sanananda.

It was a rugged walk, battered by the rain in the slippery jungle. One of the many creeks we waded through had a log stretched across it to allow footsloggers to cross the waters. I waited until the others had crossed, and then mounted the log. About halfway across, I slipped and disappeared into the creek, surfacing to wade to the other side. It was the end of my wristwatch.

We arrived at army headquarters in Sanananda at 5 pm that day and reported to the intelligence tent. It was a long tent, brimming with majors and colonels, who turned when we entered, and, without uttering a word, returned to what they were doing. We were not welcome. Syd left to cover a story behind the lines, while Cliff and I found a spot along the trail to doss down for the night. We had no idea whether we were in a safe area or not. We could hear the gunfire ahead of us, but that was not unusual. The natives made a hut of tree branches, and, as the night was setting in, we brought out the canned rations, looking forward to yet another cold beef stew. My sleep was restless, broken by noise and the hard ground. At dawn, we woke to discover the natives had disappeared. They were loath to hang around the front line, but we used their branch shack as a base from which to work until Sanananda was taken.

It was a difficult campaign to cover because most of the fighting took place at night. Furthermore, there was no definable front line because the Japanese, the Americans and the Australians were in pockets, around the trail. The fighting involved sniping, or throwing a grenade into a foxhole, so if you wandered around by yourself looking for the action, you had a good chance of being knocked over by a Japanese or an ally. Of course, we never saw many soldiers. The communication lines that crossed the jungle floor – yellow for the Japanese and green for us – was the only sign of them. According to the rules of war, neither side touched the communication lines; to do so would have caused mayhem – and who would want mayhem in a war?

So I developed a different routine in Sanananda than Buna. Every day I took off to shoot any pictures I could find, sometimes with a patrol.

One day, Cliff and I were out on a patrol with a sergeant who was laying wires for his communications unit. We came across a Japanese soldier, who had been shot and was writhing on the ground. The sergeant put his rifle to the man's head and I quickly turned away to miss the fatal shot. I don't know what Cliff did. It was the first time I had been in that position, and I did not care to watch.

Later, on the track, we were overtaken by four RAAF airmen who had been sent to look for a lost Wirraway plane that had been shot down the day before. The men had been ordered to retrieve any bodies that could be found in the wreckage, and Cliff and I thought there might be a story in it. An army jeep only has room for four men in the seats, so Cliff and I took the positions over the back wheels, where we could dangle our legs over the side.

We were heading along the track when there was a huge explosion, and we were all thrown into the air for a few surreal seconds. I landed on the side of the jeep, scraping some skin off my private parts. The rear right-hand wheel had hit a land mine, sending a piece of shrapnel up through the floor of the jeep, missing one of the airmen's legs only by inches. Cliff was the only one hurt badly, when parts of one of the wheels tore off the heel of his boot and jarred his foot, leaving him in intense pain and with his leg badly bruised.

Part II: War

The incident ended the search for the day, and I said goodbye to Cliff, who was flown out to Port Moresby for an extended hospital stay. I don't know whether they found the plane.

Chapter Six

The Carty luck

Troops on guard on the top of Shaggy Ridge, New Guinea.

IN BETWEEN CAMPAIGNS, we took our breaks in Port Moresby. One night, that same year, a few of us were sitting in our hut, a large room, that slept twenty. We had finished our evening supper and relaxed onto our stretcher beds, shooting the breeze. Heavy rain pelted down, lightning lit up the sky and thunder boomed like the bombers we listened to every day. The thunder shook our hut, and, at times, drowned out normal conversation.

Out of the din came the sound of a plane, which was obviously close because we could hear it clearly above the noise of the storm. It circled the hut, looking for the airstrip.

Flickers of History

It was certainly no night for flying, and any pilot would have found it impossible to see. One of my companions, John Quinn, wrote for *The Sun* (Sydney). He filed this story back to the newspaper telling what happened that night:

> Jack was a visitor who had just arrived from a trip he made in a barge up the coast of New Guinea, visiting villages and gathering fresh fruit from the natives to bring back to the large military hospital in Port Moresby. Jack came out of the night with water dripping from his water cape. He was drenched from the knees down.
>
> 'Filthy weather,' said Jack.
>
> Above all this noise from the storm, everybody heard the plane circling above us. It was flying mighty low.
>
> At first, the warcos were more interested in listening to Jack's stories, his hair-raising plane rides, when suddenly an uneasy tone began to enter the conversation.
>
> John was talking about a trip to Dobodura from Port Moresby when the plane roared right above us.
>
> Bill looked up and said, 'I wouldn't like to be up there tonight.' Bill's eyebrows are like a straight black bar but when he's worried, they twitch up at the ends.
>
> We were all listening. I suppose Bill has flown more than any of us. When the plane circled around, Bill said, 'that pilot is in real trouble.'
>
> His eyebrows twitched up.

Part II: War

The clouds three-hundred feet above us had blotted out the sky but the rain eased for a couple of minutes. We all raced outside and looked up. Bill muttered, 'Jeez.' We knew what he was thinking. The hills surrounding us had summits in the clouds.

We went inside again, tongue-tied, swatting mosquitoes and listening to the plane circling. Little beads of sweat stood out on all of us.

'It sounds like a transport,' said Bill.

'You can't tell in this weather,' said John.

The sound of the plane began fading.

'They'll get him in,' said Bill.

In the distance we saw a short pillar of light through our doorway.

'It's a search light,' said Bill, as we heard the sound of the plane swing towards that light. The plane had its landing lights on.

'He's jake now,' said Jack. But he wasn't. John reached for his cape.

'I'm going out onto the airstrip. Anyone coming?' He yelled for a driver.

'What's that,' screamed Jack excitedly, diving through the door. Bill ran after him. A dirty orange glow crept upwards as we heard the explosion. The glow crept up into the sky. It silhouetted a stark black hill. Then it was gone.

'I've never seen it as dark as that before,' said Jack. 'Maybe it was a flare.'

'Flares burn longer than that,' said Bill.

We waited for more than an hour for John to return. We heard John's jeep coming. He stood in the door and said, 'It was a bomber.' Jack looked outside and cursed savagely.

The clouds had gone and in the east there was another glow. The moon was rising.

The plane, which had come from Townsville, had twenty Americans on board. No one could have survived.

I followed the Allies as they moved north, pushing the Japanese out of New Guinea and away from Australia. At different times, I met up with various correspondents, reporters and cameramen but I mostly operated alone. As we moved away from Buna and Sanananda towards Lae, I travelled with a fellow warco, Bill Marion.

I had heard about Lieutenant Commander John Bulkeley long before Marion and I met the man. Bulkeley had helped MacArthur and his family escape from the Philippines in 1941, ferrying him from Corregidor down to Mindanao, so he and his family could head to Australia on board a B-17. Lieutenant Commander Bulkeley was chosen for that trip because of the bravery he had shown in past skirmishes. In his frail three-ply PT-boat operating out of Morobe on the coast of New Guinea, Bulkeley attacked Japanese warships.

Marion and I met Bulkeley over lunch in Morobe. We learned of his mission to Lae, and he welcomed us aboard. The dusk boat trip was no good to me photographically because of insufficient light, but I went along for the ride. Bulkeley, a tall, thickset good-looking bloke, was a real gentleman. Before the trip, he gave us a place to sleep and drop our gear. We left at 4 pm with two other boats following in our wake. The PT-boats were built for speed rather than strength, although they were loaded with Bofors guns, which were like long cannons. Bofors fired medium-sized shells at a rapid pace, spewing out the cases like a machine-gun in action.

The fine and calm weather made it a smooth ride. After about an hour, Bulkeley signalled to one of the other boats to break off and head further north for Finschhafen, while the remaining boat continued on behind us. Marion and I stood chatting beside Bulkeley as he kept the boat on a smooth twelve knots. As we rode into the danger zone, he cut the speed to four knots and put the mufflers on to stifle some of the noise. As darkness set in, we approached our destination. We were whispering when a barrage of shells fired from the beach exploded around us. Marion and I hit the deck, grabbing a stanchion in utter fear. With my camera in my right hand, I hung on for dear life with my other hand.

In a flash, Bulkeley brought the speed up from four knots to fifty-two knots, and, under concentrated fire, he played cat-and-mouse with the Japanese, zigzagging at breakneck speed while yelling to see if we were okay. It was impossible to hear any replies over the Japanese shells landing around us. Every time a shell exploded, a short burst of light followed, illuminating the whole sky like a string of firecrackers.

A Japanese plane zoomed overhead and dropped a flare that illuminated the whole sky. At that moment, I thought we were gone, but Bulkeley refused to give up. Even with the help of a flare, he was a hard target to hit, as the Japanese pilot discovered when he dived towards us with guns blazing. Bullets landed all around us in the water, and it would have taken only one to hit the arsenal on board to set off a chain of explosions that would have blown us out of the water. With machine guns proving ineffective, the pilot dropped a bomb that landed just behind the boat. Again, he failed. Sweating profusely, and with my teeth clenched, I prayed to God that all of us would survive. I had my camera in my hand, but did not get a single shot of footage – such is the price of self-preservation.

The ordeal seemed like hours, but it lasted about fifteen minutes. Bulkeley ferried us to safety, slowing down to a more reasonable speed. I remembered the stories I had been told about this man, and my own experience confirmed them. He had handled the boat with such skill, and showed leadership and courage under intense fire. His cool determination got us out of that situation without a bullet hole in the boat or ourselves.

My trek with Marion continued to be punctuated with extraordinary people. I sent back stories on most of them but never saw the results in the picture theatres at home. Leslie 'Bull' Allen, known as the gentle giant, was one of these people. Corporal Allen was an Australian stretcher-bearer, based at Mount Tambu. Allen was a huge man with obvious physical and emotional strength, perhaps borne of a difficult childhood. He told me he grew up with his mother and sister in Adelaide. One day his mother took them both into the city and asked them to wait on a street corner while she attended to some business. She never returned. At twelve, Allen assumed responsibility for his younger sister and himself.

Part II: War

His compassion was evident in the battlefield, where he carried wounded American and Australian soldiers from the danger zones. The Americans were engaged on the beach at the foot of Mount Tambu in late July 1943. During heavy fighting on 30 July, Allen risked his life to save a dozen wounded. The Australians had just about wiped out the Japanese in the Salamaua area at the top of Mount Tambu, but they were running short of rations. The Americans admired Allen so much that they told him to take what he wanted for his soldiers. Allen hoisted two large boxes on his shoulders and each day climbed the steep track up to the top of Mount Tambu. He made the climb with such ease, it was as though he was walking on level ground. I filmed him doing the trek a number of times, but I had to ask him to slow down so I could take the pictures.

The Americans awarded him with a Silver Star 'for gallantry in action', and the Australians gave him a Military Medal for rescuing so many of his comrades. He was hailed a hero, and, when he received the awards, stories of his courage on the front line and his contribution to the war effort appeared in the press. It was at this time that his mother made contact for the first time since she abandoned him and his sister. Allen refused her request for money.

Like so many other people I met during the war, I did not find out how his story ended. For me, he will always be that gigantic man striding up Mount Tambu like he was on a Sunday jaunt.

To be in the middle of the action is what matters to a cameraman. The most captivating footage is always that which

Flickers of History

has been shot at close range, especially in those days before the long-range lens. So when a public relations officer from the Australian Army told the press corps that they would have to wait on the ship rather than land with the troops at Lae in September 1943, I dismissed it as a ridiculous order.

We were aboard a fleet of rocket ships, known as LCIs (Landing Craft, Infantry). These craft were used to land large numbers of troops by dropping stairways down onto a beach the moment they touch the shore. The fleet lined up next to each other, with their bows resting along the beach. As the troops prepared to move off the ship, I cursed the public relations officer and sat astride a rail on the last of the line of LCIs, positioning my camera to get the best possible footage from the boat. Out of nowhere, a Japanese plane headed directly towards the beach, flying in line with the row of ships. My camera followed the troops, who were already jumping on the beach. As I saw the plane, I slid onto the deck, maintaining my camera on the rail with my finger on the trigger.

The plane dropped its bomb just before it skimmed over the top of my ship. It hit the second last LCI in the row, the one next to mine. The bomb exploded on impact, killing eight Australian soldiers. I turned the camera onto the burning deck of the ship as all the LCIs, including the bombed one, began reversing out of the beach, with their troops unloaded.

The army planned to take the ships back to Buna, where the troops were originally loaded, with the correspondents. The warcos, who were fuming by this stage, would then be put onto another convoy that would return to Lae. Only then would they be allowed onto the beach.

I knew nothing of this plan. My own plan was to head back to headquarters to try to fix a toothache, which was giving me hell. On the way back, a PR officer told me that I should be on the convoy to Lae; I raced back to the beach just in time to see the last LST (Landing Ship, Tank) disappearing into the distance. It was turning out to be a bad day.

I spotted a PT-boat being repaired on the beach, and the American captain assured me that if he ever got the boat repaired, he was heading back to his base in Morobe, which was on the way to Lae. I asked him if he would take me, on the off-chance we might catch up with the convoy. Three hours later, we headed off.

The Carty luck was in because, just off the coast near Morobe, the last LST was in view. We had no trouble catching the ship, which had a top speed of eight knots, and the crew got my gear onto the boat while I jumped aboard.

After fending off an attack by a lone Japanese plane, the convoy landed at midnight, and, in total darkness, we made our way off the boat and up the beach. Wire had been laid across the beach to help the tanks travel through the sand. As I jumped off the boat and ran towards the jungle, I went head over heels, and my film flew off into the darkness. Knowing I could not get any more for at least twenty-four hours, I began frantically scratching around in the sand to find it. Suddenly, a tank loomed out of nowhere but, fortunately, I was thrown out of its path by a soldier. Nothing more could be done until morning, so I found a spot in the sand to sleep for the night and dozed off.

The next morning, the beach was awash with boxes containing an odd variety of wartime supplies, including wine glasses and tins of fruit. I filled my bags up, having not seen tinned fruit for months. Later, a couple of soldiers were arrested by Australian Military Police after they were caught doing the same thing.

I advanced with the troops after sending my message for supply of film. There was no hurry because we were pinned down as I waited for my supplies, which arrived three days later. There was a race of sorts between the Australian 7th and 9th Divisions to see which could get into Lae first. One warco, a bloke named Alan Dawes, who wrote for the *Argus*, was with me at the time. He was a funny guy – a big rotund man with a handlebar moustache – and a great writer, who always maintained his sense of humour. I had first met him in Darwin, where he used to get drunk and stand stark naked on a table eating whole cans of sheep's tongue. He loved sheep's tongue.

We were in the middle of the jungle, pinned down with the troops, as planes flew overhead, shooting everything to pieces. It was as hot as Hades, so Dawes wore no shirt. As the planes passed overhead, we all dived under a log for cover. I heard cursing and swearing and turned to see his legs sticking out from under a log. Dawes was getting eaten alive by ants. It was one of those funny moments that breaks out of a serious situation. I laughed when I saw his article on the landing finished with the words, 'but I was the last into Lae'.

The battle for Shaggy Ridge in November–December 1943 became the backdrop for Australia's first and only two-reel documentary, *Jungle Patrol*. Audiences at home got to know the

Part II: War

talents of a battle-scarred battalion of Australian soldiers, including Horse, Red and Shorty, through that twenty-minute newsreel, which was nominated for an Oscar in the category of documentary. The editor-in-chief of Associated Press, Tom Gurr, took time off to write the script and direct the film without pay. I was field manager in New Guinea at the time, and chief cameraman on that film.

Shaggy Ridge was a huge mountain, topped with a rocky peak, which could only be reached by a narrow path hugging the side of the cliff face. The peak, known to us as the Pimple, was held by the Japanese and it took an Australian battalion close to two months to take the top because the path left our soldiers vulnerable to sniper fire. It was only after the RAAF bombed the pimple that the Australians could make an effective raid on the peak. When the mission was completed, we discovered the bodies of the eight Japanese soldiers who had kept our troops at bay. Topography had been on their side.

The battle for that hill was not the only battle in town. I had a few fights to contend with myself, especially with my fellow cameraman and former mentor, Bill Trerise. I had first worked with Trerise during the Cinesound days, when I got my start through Walter Sully. At the beginning of the war, Bill had been chief cameraman at Movietone, but he was fired in 1943 because of a disagreement with the manager. I recommended Trerise to Jack Allen, the manager of the DOI. As Tom and I prepared to shoot *Jungle Patrol* (1944), Trerise landed in New Guinea.

'I suppose they've told you,' Trerise said to me when he arrived. I didn't know what he was talking about. 'I'm chief cameraman,' he told me. 'Pig's arse,' was my reply. I had been in New Guinea for almost a year, and had the contacts and the experience in wartime conditions, Trerise had only just arrived. Unless told otherwise by Jack Allen, we were equal. But Jack refused to buy into the argument, so began a war between the two cameramen.

As it turned out, I spent most of my time on patrols with the troops, while Trerise sat on top of Shaggy Ridge shooting cutaways, the footage that goes in between the main action sequences. When I needed to shoot the air force attacks and asked to borrow his swing-lens camera, a newer model than my own supplied by the department, Trerise refused.

Despite the office politics, the film was a great success, achieving worldwide release. *Smith's Weekly* said the film 'makes you sit on the edge of your seat', and that it ranked 'with anything the war has produced'. At a Pitt Street theatre in Sydney, it was advertised as *Jungle Patrol*, shot by Bill Carty. A friend took a picture, so I could see the billboard. Trerise was furious, but I was secretly delighted.

I was bright yellow when I returned to Australia for my second leave. The malaria tablets kept the sickness at bay, but they turned us canary yellow. People used to ask what made us so yellow. We flippantly replied, 'the war' – we were scared yellow.

Six months made no difference to my relationship with my daughter Pauline. She still screamed the house down when I came near. I took Mary and the baby down to Canberra to shoot a story, thinking the extra time with her might help, but it was not an easy trip. It was frustrating to have a small child who didn't want anything to do with me. At least it provided Mary with a break.

I was called back to New Guinea as soon as I returned from Canberra. I flew out of Rose Bay, close to our house, on board a Sunderland aircraft. In good conditions, the flying boats were great to travel on, especially over long distances. Leaving Australia for New Guinea, the planes would fly only two hundred feet above the water. This was wonderful on a calm, clear day but shocking on a windy, stormy one. Any disturbance bumped them around like a ship at sea, leaving all but the toughest passengers airsick. Unfortunately, I was not the toughest of flyers, and suffered airsickness on a number of occasions.

As I stood on the pier at Rose Bay, I was delighted to see the calm conditions on the water. Mary and our three children made the familiar trip to say goodbye. We were joined by Vincent Tubbs, a handsome black American correspondent, who worked for the black newspapers in the US. Dressed in an officer's uniform, he looked striking. He was also a talented writer, who was well respected among the warcos.

I introduced Vincent to my family, and Jim's eyes grew wider and wider. He stared at Vincent, before blurting out, 'Dad, what's the matter with his skin?' Jim had never seen a black man before. Most of the American soldiers were posted elsewhere, so there were not many black men on the streets of Sydney. Mary and I were shocked and embarrassed, but Vincent just smiled, as calm as ever. 'Don't worry, not to mind,' he said. Mary began apologising, but Vincent stopped her. 'Forget about it.'

Chapter Seven

Chaplains

Missionaries just after their release from the Japanese in New Guinea.

I'M NO SAINT, but I have always tried to be a good Catholic. As I watched men in battle, committing the most extraordinary acts in the name of war, I never lost my faith – it only became stronger. When soldiers were faced with their own fear of death, their thoughts most often turned to God, even those who would have professed no religion only days before. These men were capable of achieving seemingly impossible feats. And from the days in Darwin to the battles in the Pacific, through to the surrender on the *USS Missouri* and the occupation of Japan, one group of men stood out in my memory – the chaplains.

Flickers of History

They were at the forefront of every major battle, comforting the wounded, giving the last rites to the dying, and burying the dead. Men killed in battle were dragged from the swamps to a dry patch of ground for burial. The first Australian I saw buried in battle was a sergeant who spoke Japanese; he died during the battle for Shaggy Ridge. Frequently he would walk up to the dividing line on the ridge, which was about three-feet wide, so he could call out to the Japanese, urging them to surrender rather than fight and die. During the battle, he was hit by a sniper and rolled down the steep side of the mountain. His body was recovered days later, after the Australians had taken the territory. On a bleak and rainy morning, he was buried on top of Shaggy Ridge, accompanied by the prayers of an Australian chaplain, and laid in a hole, with a blanket over his face. As his comrades shovelled dirt over his body, I wondered what passed through their young minds. Those men had seen the sergeant alive only a short time before. Ninety per cent of men killed in all wars are aged between eighteen and twenty-five.

On that occasion, the chaplain was Catholic, but the prayer was the same for everyone. Often there was little time to discover the religion of a dead soldier – besides, in war, all religions seem to meld into one. It was said during the First World War that every soldier killed on the field of battle would go straight to God. In that war, all chaplains became known as padres, no matter what their religion, and, in both world wars, they served as camp counsellors. Even those who boasted of having no religion sought comfort from the padres. The Australian and American armies treated chaplains differently.

Part II: War

Both forces gave them a rank, from lieutenant to general, but the Australians, regardless of their rank, had more freedom than the American chaplains. The high-ranking Australian officers treated the chaplains with greater respect and dignity than the American top brass. American officers often pulled rank on a low-ranking padre, who had to obey orders like any junior officer. An American chaplain, ranked a major, told me that the Australian chaplains faced far less red tape and could roam through the battle areas.

Father Joseph Whelan, an inspiring American Catholic padre, brought comfort to many men. Ranked a captain, he received full support from his supervising colonel, a Protestant. Father Whelan had served in the Far East for three years before volunteering for service in New Guinea, where he had freedom to move with the men through the jungles of Buna. His warmth and friendliness drew me to him. A tall man with a long angular face, Father Whelan had a quiet way about him, which provided a great source of strength to those in trouble. He was not interested in the limelight that my camera provided; the chaplain was too retiring for that.

Every evening, if it were at all possible, he used to say mass on a makeshift table set up somewhere behind the front line in the jungle. An army assistant helped him with his duties. I tried to make it to each service.

One night, we sat in the coconut grove not far from the front line in Buna, where Father Whelan had set up for mass. His sermons were kept short because of the danger of sitting in the middle of the battlefield. The padre offered a prayer of comfort for those lucky enough to make it through the day's battle. At the end of his prayer, the padre urged the boys to return to the same spot the following night for mass. As he uttered those words, a hail of bullets shattered the stillness, clipping the trees above the heads of the men. Looking up, Father Whelan smiled and said, 'God willing.' His wry smile relaxed the men. He appeared to be invincible, protected by God, as shrapnel ripped apart the leaves around him.

The padre also had the gruesome task of picking up the bodies for burial in a common grave. I followed him with a camera one day, witnessing the horror of an act that had become routine. The intensity of battle and the jungle climate often meant that the remains were little more than bones. Father Whelan collected and buried the bodies of all soldiers, without regard to their religious allegiances, using the same prayer. To the padre, they were all God's children, to be received by their creator.

Father Whelan was an inspirational man. He took time out in Sydney to visit my family, and my son Jim, only three at the time, was particularly affected by him, recalling his influence as profound and citing him as one of the reasons he joined the priesthood. Father Whelan was very tall, with a deep soothing voice, and he had a natural affinity with children. Our family home became a refuge for visiting clergy, both in Australia and during the occupation in Japan. The Australian priests sent up to Japan after the war had their first Christmas dinner at our house.

The jungle fighting took its toll on Father Whelan, who suffered many bouts of malaria during his three years in the combat zone. He returned to the States before the end of the war to raise money to build a church in his home town,

Owosso, in Shiawassee County. The church, St Paul's, was finally completed with his motto: 'Never turn anybody in trouble away.' He certainly lived up to those words in the jungle. We kept in touch until he died in 1973.

Father Francis Cosgrove, an Australian Redemptorist missioner who had been working in the Philippines since 1932, became the subject of one of my newsreels. I met him there in July 1945, late in the war, when it was becoming harder to find stories to captivate home audiences. We were just waiting for the invasion of Japan, which, we were told, was planned for October that year. I took a jeep with a driver and headed out of town. I had no idea where we were going or what we would find. We came upon La Salle Catholic Chapel, where we met a battle-scarred Father Cosgrove. Bullets had pockmarked the walls in his little chapel, and the altar had been destroyed. The padre began his story.

In February of that year, as he offered his daily mass before fifteen brothers of the college and forty Filipino parishioners, a group of Japanese soldiers burst into the church and began spraying bullets around the altar. Hit in the first burst, Father Cosgrove fell on the altar steps. At first he could not move, paralysed by the burning bullets in his legs and upper body. The Japanese left believing the whole congregation was dead. But they were known for returning to the scene to ensure no one survived. Father Cosgrove knew he must remain conscious and hide himself in case they returned.

With every move causing excruciating pain to his torn body, Father Cosgrove crawled over the dead, praying that he could conceal himself before the soldiers returned. He could not

Flickers of History

remember how long it took him to hide. With the last of his energy, he crawled underneath two bodies and hid most of his upper body.

In the morning, the Japanese returned, looking for any sign of life. Not wanting to waste bullets, they used bayonets to finish off any survivors. Father felt the cold steel of the bayonet drive into his exposed legs several times. He could never explain how he remained still. The soldiers left, satisfied there were no survivors. In intense agony, Father Whelan lay under the bodies for another four days.

American soldiers discovered Father Cosgrove and took him to a medical centre. He was touched by the treatment he received from the troops and wrote a letter of appreciation to the US government:

> The fidelity of so many members of the American forces to their religious duties has been a source of great edification, not only to me personally, but to all priests in the Philippines. The present mission in La Salle College, Manila, is an expression of my gratitude to the heroic troops who rescued me from what seemed like certain death. You have just reason to be proud of your sons, husbands, or daughters in the armed forces. May God continue to protect these sterling and gallant youths! May they return to you soon, chastened by suffering but ennobled by trials.
>
> Sincerely in Christ,
> Father Cosgrove
> July 22, 1945.

Part II: War

Father Sheridan, a Maryknoll missioner in charge of the La Salle Chapel, explained the contribution of the mission: 'Every Sunday over 1000 military personnel attend Mass. The missionary value of their practical Catholicity can be measured only in heaven.'

I sent the newsreel back to America, with interviews of Father Cosgrove and footage of his chapel, showing where he was cut down by fire and where he lay for four days. I was particularly moved by his story, not only because of my Catholic faith. It showed the tenacity of the human spirit.

Chapter Eight

Paramount

Bob Hope entertains the troops on Noemfoor Island, 1944. Bill Carty covered Hope's visit to the island.

'HEY CARTY, how'd you like to work for Paramount News?' asked Earl Crotchett. 'Try me,' I replied. Crotchett covered for the American pool of Paramount, Pathe News of the Day, Universal and Fox Movietone, which were all based in New York. I had met him after Buna, and he asked me about the job in 1943. The Australian cameraman Damien Parer had already left DOI to join Paramount, and was being moved from the South-West to the Central Pacific. There would be a position vacant.

Flickers of History

I knew Paramount paid much more than the Australian government. The Americans received US$12.50 a day, with a US$25 000 life-insurance policy, while we were paid thirteen pounds a week, with three guineas expenses.

Crotchett told me to cable Paramount, and 'just tell them you are prepared to accept the job.' I did so, at great expense, and six weeks later I got a reply. They wanted to know more about me. Through surface mail, which slowed the process considerably, I wrote to tell them what I had done. I didn't hear anything more until Parer was killed in Peleliu, near Guam, in 1944.

When Mary received the letter, I was in the jungle and she couldn't reach me for some time. She had heard about Parer's death, and told Paramount she did not want me going over to them to get killed. 'We don't want any dead cameramen either,' replied the Paramount representative.

As my job offer sat in the mail at headquarters in Hollandia, I accompanied the troops in campaigns around Morotai and Noemfoor Island. I had joined the spotters in their Piper Cub, a two-seater single-engine plane usually used in reconnaissance, but which was employed directing the artillery towards their Japanese targets. Fired from the ground, the shells traced an arc over our tiny plane as they made their way towards the Japanese back on the ground. While it was frightening to be in the middle of such action, I had no choice but to place my trust in our artillerymen.

After the Allies drove the Japanese out of Noemfoor in 1944, Bob Hope flew in with his entourage to entertain the troops. He arrived in a Black Widow, a night-flying plane, with another comedian, Jerry Colonna, and a band of showgirls. I followed them around the island for their tour and show – the trip lasted less than a day. The show was pretty good, considering we had been hard up for entertainment for the past few years. Hope was funny, and the girls went down well with the audience of three to four thousand battle-weary men. When the army showed the entertainers around the island, I climbed in Colonna's jeep. I don't know what it was like with Bob Hope, but there were certainly no jokes in our jeep. I couldn't get a word out of the guy; he just sat there with a silly grin on his face.

In Morotai, I shot another documentary called *Island Target* (1945) about the RAAF raid on a Japanese-held island, before dropping back to Hollandia. I finally made it to headquarters, where I found a stack of mail from Mary and from Paramount. I immediately replied to Paramount with a big yes.

When I returned to Sydney to complete the negotiations, DOI threatened to put me in the army. Although I had been called up in 1941, my work as a DOI cameraman meant I didn't have to join the army, so I had more freedom than a regular soldier. The Minister for Information, Arthur Calwell, the man who replaced Senator Ashley, was a little more understanding than his underlings. He seemed like a nice old guy. 'We don't want you to go and photograph the Americans,' he told me. 'It's not about that,' I responded. 'This is the biggest job I've ever had, and I've got a family to keep.' The minister finally agreed and said he would make a statement to the press about my new job. Parer had left amid great controversy, so he did not want that to happen again.

Flickers of History

When I went onto the Paramount payroll, my salary tripled. My first destination was Guam, and I jumped on board a C-47, which flew straight into a typhoon – I did not think we would make it. We were forced to stop off in Peleliu to refuel. It was a strange coincidence because Parer was killed and buried there in September 1944, just a couple of months before, and here I was going to do his job.

I was given navy accreditation at the Guam base for the US Seventh Fleet and was set to go on a flat top – US aircraft carrier – when I was recalled to General MacArthur's headquarters in Manila. Those who had organised my trip were annoyed, but I had no choice.

The reason for the urgent change was to get two hundred feet of tight head shots of MacArthur. It was an example of the administrative side of the job, which, at times, overrode the coverage of the actual war. 'It's time we had a good look at this guy,' the cable read. Up until this point, the European war had assumed precedence over the Pacific as far as the news desk was concerned. MacArthur was looming large in war strategy, and the ordinary man and woman did not know what he looked like. The news desk did not know how much MacArthur disliked posing for pictures. If he was going about his business in public, he did not mind being photographed, but he was not a man who would drop everything to give you a profile shot. MacArthur's public relations officer, General Le Grande Diller, warned me, 'You know it won't be easy. I don't think the old man will agree to it.' Diller promised to try, and disappeared into MacArthur's inner sanctum. He was not there long before he came out with a short answer: 'No.'

I tried a different approach. MacArthur had lunch every day with his doctor, Lieutenant Colonel Roger Egeberg. Roger agreed to ask, but he was not prepared for the answer. On the phone that afternoon, Roger told me, 'You almost got me thrown out of the goddamned car.' MacArthur popped a fuse when he mentioned my name. Roger went on, 'He said, "I already told Carty, I won't pose. End of request."' I cabled New York, but they did not understand the constraints. My boss asked, 'What gives with this guy?'

MacArthur was on his way to the Borneo operation, and I requested to go on board a cruiser, the USS *Boise*. I was one of five allowed to travel with the general on the ship, which stopped off at a number of front-line areas in the Philippines on the way to Borneo. We visited various US combat units, which were still in battle. At one stop, we rode by jeep one hundred miles from the port into the battle zone. MacArthur, who was sixty-four, seemed to fare best out of his team during the tiring journey.

The following day, I gave it one last shot. General Eichelberger was on board, so I gave him the history, and asked him as a favour to sway the general. If anybody could persuade MacArthur, Bob could, and he agreed to give it a go. Later that morning, I got the phone call. 'Be up on the captain's deck at 1400 hours,' said Bob. I thanked him profusely.

I arrived ten minutes early and set up my camera on the deck. Bang on time, MacArthur stepped out of the captain's cabin, smoking his corncob pipe. 'What would you like me to do, Carty?' I asked him to pace up and down the deck twice, then pause alongside the camera. He did just that, giving me the requested two hundred feet of close-ups. 'Is that all you want?' asked the general. It was a miraculous change. I never found out what Bob said to make him alter his stance.

The next morning we reached Labuan, in North Borneo. MacArthur stood beside the heavy guns as they pounded the beach. He remained still, unfazed by the noise that vibrated the core of my body. I had great trouble steadying my camera.

MacArthur was transported to the beach. A gaggle of brass, including admirals and generals, followed MacArthur to the beach. It formed the biggest gathering of senior military officers I had ever seen. The Australian troops on the beach stood in amazement. They kept asking, 'Where's Blamey? in reference to their own general whom they had not seen in the Pacific campaign.

Small-arms fire whizzed around us as MacArthur strode up to the front line, pausing a few steps away from no-man's-land. The Australian troops looked on in awe as MacArthur talked to the soldiers for around twenty minutes.

Although we didn't know it at the time, the assault on Balikpapan, in July 1945, was to be our last major campaign in the Pacific. We were now based in Manila with the American brass and a meeting confirmed the assault would use the LCIs as rocket ships for the first time. I was granted permission to ride on one of the ships to film the assault on the beach. The colonel in charge of the rocket convoy was a bit of a crackpot; he was forever scratching his neck, as if he had a dreadful skin complaint. But he wanted me to be on his

Part II: War

ship, and made arrangements to transfer me onto the lead ship the night before the landing.

I spent the night on another ship and got on quite well with the captain. It was a pretty rough night, as there was no bed for me, so I slept, or tried to sleep, down below deck, where the rockets were stored. I figured, if I died now, I would go in one hell of a hurry.

The ships had to pick their way through a minefield in the water the next morning. As the convoy travelled past the danger zone towards its destination, the captain of my ship was ordered to take me at full speed to the colonel's ship. I told him not to bother, that it would make no difference, but the colonel insisted and the captain refused to disobey orders. Troops on the other ships were confused when our ship broke out of the convoy at full speed to reach the lead ship. I jumped over to the colonel's ship, where I was told I would have complete freedom to film once the attack began. I remembered the fuss made by the Australian public relations officer during the Lae landing.

Planes had already bombed the beach from 6 am. The LCIs were converted to rocket ships, and huge racks were attached to the side of each vessel to hold rocket shells. The ships lined up, side by side, fifty yards away from each other. The vessels were to move towards the beach in the same formation and fire when the captain of each ship gave the order.

I stood only a few feet away from the rocket racks when the firing began, one hundred yards out from the beach. I always jumped when the big guns were fired, but the noise and the heat off the rockets overwhelmed me – I thought I might cook. The symmetry of the ships, moving and firing towards the beach, produced a magnificent picture. I also took great shots of the rockets exploding in flames as they hit the beach. These were some of the most graphic pictures I took during the war.

Three times, the rocket ships backed off, reloaded and fired before the troops were sent in on barges, led by General MacArthur. As we got to the beach, shots were coming in and everyone hit the sand except MacArthur. Again, his invincibility astounded me.

I followed MacArthur up the beach, where we came upon some dead Japanese. 'There's a good Jap,' he said, as I filmed a body from the ground before panning up to the general. MacArthur stayed on the front line with his troops for about twenty minutes.

After the assault, I prepared to return to Manila on an amphibious plane, a PBY-40, which had been loaded with so much equipment that it was in danger of not getting off the ground on the short runway. The pilot told the four passengers to move to the tail of the plane, wait for his signal, then run up towards the pilot. This would allow him to use the weight to keep the plane balanced for the lift-off. The method only just worked, and we cleared the treetops. Eventually we landed on the water to take more baggage from a barge. It seemed foolhardy at the time, but the vast expanse of water gave the plane an endless space for take off, and there was no problems when we eventually got back into the air. It reminded me, though, that the risks during wartime were not only on the front line.

Chapter Nine

Surrender

General Douglas MacArthur signs the Surrender Document aboard the US battleship Missouri *to seal the closing of the war. Photograph: US Navy.*

AFTER BALIKPAPAN, there was a feeling that, militarily, Japan remained the only place left to go. General MacArthur, with his team of commanders, settled down in Manila to plan the invasion of Japan, due to take place in October 1945. It was expected to be the bloodiest and most costly of all the Pacific campaigns, in terms of human lives and resources. Intelligence gathered by headquarters suggested Japanese soldiers planned to fight street by street, regardless of the human toll, as their supreme sacrifice. The Japanese people were equally terrified about what to expect from their enemy. Their leaders had told them children would be slaughtered, and women would be raped and then killed. No one would be spared. We were convinced it would be a bloodbath for our side too, for our boys knew first-hand the tenacity of the Japanese soldier.

In the meantime, though, close to two hundred warcos were bored stiff. Most of us lived in a big house in Rizal Avenue, Manila, but, as we waited for the invasion, an influx of new correspondents meant the house could no longer hold the press corps. We were shifted to huts in the army headquarters, where we sat around doing little apart from getting a suntan. While major strategy consumed the generals, we had nothing to film. The American warcos took advantage of the daily shuttle of planes to and from the States. They could hitch a ride quite easily, allowing them to see their family and friends, but I had access to no such service. Australia was no longer so important as an American war room, and, consequently, I had not seen my family for six months. I had to write instead. Mary wondered about our future, but I couldn't tell her because I didn't know myself.

While invasion plans continued, US President Harry Truman and his closest advisers worked on how to bring the war to an abrupt end through unconventional means – the first atomic bomb. There were four targets for the bomb, Hiroshima, Kokura, Niigata and Nagasaki. The old capital of Kyoto and the new capital Tokyo, were ruled out, even though the latter had already been extensively bombed with conventional weapons. After much debate, Hiroshima and Nagasaki were chosen for strategic reasons. Both housed major military installations and industrial complexes and both fed major naval ports. Furthermore, there were no prisoner of war camps near Hiroshima.

At 8.15 am on 6 August 1945, Colonel Paul Tibbets, Commander of the 509th Group, dropped the first atomic bomb from the B-29 *Enola Gay*, which had been named after his mother. The target was Hiroshima, on the main island of Honshu. Just how many people perished as a result of the bomb is impossible to say. Initially it was thought to be about 70 000, but the true figure is at least double that. More than 60 per cent of the city was destroyed.

The news broke in the correspondents' camp that day via the US Army newspaper. At the time, we were convinced that MacArthur was completely in the dark, though reports since have suggested he knew of the bomb in advance. As for the correspondents, we didn't even know what an atomic bomb was, and consequently knew nothing about the attack.

Those warcos still in the States were in a panic, as most had not notified their offices they were away from headquarters. Many had not even told their families they were in the country, preferring to see Hollywood instead. I received several cables from cameramen asking me not to divulge their whereabouts to their office, giving them time to jump on the first plane back to Manila. They needn't have worried about missing the Japanese surrender – even with the atomic bomb, it wasn't forthcoming. Despite Truman's statement warning that 'a rain of ruin from the air, the like of which has never been seen on this earth', would follow, Japan would not accept defeat.

When the second bomb was dropped on Nagasaki, the Japanese acknowledged the war was over and it was left to MacArthur to negotiate the terms of surrender. Communique number 1228 from the General Headquarters of the Southwest Pacific Area on 15 August 1945 consisted of two lines: 'The Japanese capitulation having been announced, no further formal communiques will be issued from this headquarters.'

MacArthur played no part in the negotiations that brought about Japan's surrender, but, as the newly appointed Supreme Commander of the Allied Powers, he was responsible for organising the surrender ceremony and occupation of Japan.

Sixteen emissaries, representatives of the Emperor of Japan, reached Manila on 19 August to negotiate the terms of surrender. MacArthur had prepared the armistice documents but he sent Lieutenant General Richard Sutherland, his chief of staff, to conduct the conference. The Japanese were led by Lieutenant General Torashiro Kawabe, vice-chief of the Army General Staff. Emperor Hirohito's orders regarding the delegation, released through the Allied army public relations office, said nothing of the defeat of Japan; the Emperor merely gave authorisation for these men 'to make on behalf of ourselves any arrangements directed by the Supreme Commander of the Allied Powers'.

The Japanese were transported in a special plane, painted white with green markings, so that it would be recognised by both sides. The Allied forces sent out an escort of a dozen American fighters when the plane was two hundred miles out of Manila to protect the delegation not only from over-zealous Allied planes but also from the possibility of the infamous

Part II: War

Kamikaze pilots. The flight went smoothly, and the plane landed on the strip in front of the army and press contingents. The tall stairs were wheeled to the plane door, and I waited to film the emissaries, who appeared proud and confident in spite of the task ahead. The army men were dressed in full military regalia, with swords swinging by their sides and pistols shining in their holsters.

I got my pictures and left, heading for army headquarters before the delegation arrived there, so I could shoot some more film. The men were greeted at headquarters by an officer who requested they remove their weapons – ceremonial or otherwise – before entering the conference room. It served as a reminder that this was no ordinary diplomatic event. The Japanese looked dejected – perhaps because they took the request as an insult – but they had no alternative, and, reluctantly, removed the offending items.

Only two cameramen were allowed in the conference room – me and a US Army cameraman. The Japanese sat around a huge polished wooden table, with Sutherland and his staff facing them. I took close-ups of all the participants before being asked to leave so that the negotiations could commence. After the meeting, nothing was released to the waiting media. After spending nineteen hours in Manila, the Japanese were simply escorted back to their plane and returned to Japan.

The biggest story was always going to be the arrival of the first enemy force on Japanese soil in the country's history. There were close to five hundred international press representatives clamouring to get into Japan on the first plane. MacArthur's public relations officer, General Diller, took his life in his hands when he told an angry press pack that only five correspondents would be allowed to go in with the top brass.

Correspondents called a meeting, and General Diller addressed the group. We all fought to defend our own patch. I told him I had followed MacArthur around the Pacific from Melbourne, and was accredited to the US government. After telling him I would cable the president of the newsreel pool if I could not get into Japan on the first day, Diller eventually relented.

We were all ranked according to the time spent covering the war and miles done with MacArthur. That gave me number one priority, making me one of the few to arrive on a 'fatcat' plane, a DC-4, on the first day of the 'invasion of Japan'. The majority of the press corps had to travel by ship, which got them in after the first landing.

The official surrender was to take place on 2 September 1945, on board the USS *Missouri*, but Allied forces had to begin planning the event and subsequent occupation as soon as possible. The officers and support troops who would govern Japan, and a small press contingent, would board DC-4 troop-carrying planes at Okinawa and fly into Atsugi airstrip near Yokohama a few weeks before the official surrender.

As part of the first wave entering Japan, warcos were issued strict instructions and warnings that anyone who disobeyed these orders would lose accreditation and be sent home immediately. We were not allowed to leave the airstrip until General MacArthur arrived. All correspondents were issued with .45 automatic pistols and were told to make no contact with the Japanese and cause no incidents.

The issue of guns marked a departure from previous wartime policy for correspondents, who were forbidden to carry arms of any kind (even though the policy was often broken). No one knew how the Japanese would react to the enemy presence. We were told the Japanese believed that, even though the war had ended, we would kill all men, women and children. As far as we knew, they were planning to fight the invading force with every means possible. If this were the case, we had to be prepared to use our weapons in defence.

Never before in the history of the war were five hundred DC-4 planes gathered in the one spot, as were those preparing to take in the occupational forces on that first day, 30 August 1945. It made a magnificent picture for my camera.

The first plane took off from Okinawa at 1 am, while our plane left twenty minutes late. I flew with the Signal Corps camera crew, which had use of a DC-4 belonging to the Secretary of State, Edward Stettinius. It was a luxurious job, fitted with lounges and anything else one could want in the sky. I had the ultimate armchair ride into Japan. We flew over the country at around 5 am that morning and touched down an hour later. All passengers were ordered out so that the aircraft could move off the strip for the next plane to land. Aircraft arrived every three minutes.

When General MacArthur stepped off his plane at about 2 pm, he was met by General Eichelberger and me. He paused at the top of the stairs. Placing his trademark corncob pipe in his mouth, he strode down the steps to shake

Flickers of History

Eichelberger's hand, and said, 'Bob, it's been a long time, but we finally made it.'

I commandeered a vehicle with a Japanese driver and, together with three other correspondents, set out to see the damage. The main street in Tokyo, known as the Ginza, was desolate and some of the buildings were in ruins. The only women and children we saw fled at the approach of an American, while Japanese soldiers turned their backs and walked away.

We drove around the Emperor's Palace, where only one building was slightly damaged. I was looking for the *Nippon Times*, the Japanese English newspaper, to find any Japanese war film, but no one could help me. The US Army later confiscated all the film shot by the Japanese during the war.

That first night, MacArthur stayed at the New Grand Hotel in Yokohama with his mate, Skinny Wainwright, whom he had left behind in Manila. We also headed back to Yokohama, where we discovered our temporary accommodation was a cot in the Rising Sun Petroleum building, which was rough and cold. The other correspondents were scattered around in similar buildings, untouched by the bombing. More permanent living quarters would come after the official surrender. A Japanese hotel had been taken over, and army cooks installed to feed the soldiers and correspondents.

The next morning, we planned to head out again to film. The Japanese driver spotted me as I walked towards the motor pool and waved frantically – like me, he assumed we could drive around to see more of the devastation. We were wrong.

An American guard stepped in front of me, and, pointing a rifle and bayonet towards my gut, said, 'Don't touch that vehicle.' Army brass had given special orders that there were no vehicles to be given to anyone except army personnel with orders and a pass. I didn't have a pass, of course, so I had zero chance of getting out alone in the next seven days to cover stories. I was left to the mercy of army public relations.

The army provided a truck to take a group of correspondents to a prison camp in Yokohama. Two days before the Americans landed, planes, known as the Biscuit Bombers, dropped barrels stuffed full of clothes, candy bars, cookies and other food for the prisoners. The Japanese guards had walked out of the prisons on news of their surrender, leaving the prisoners free to come and go as they pleased. Freedom and food was more than the captives could bear – they gorged themselves as they related stories of how they had been beaten and starved.

I was talking to General Eichelberger when a dejected-looking soldier with one leg missing approached us on crutches. He had been wounded in the leg, and he told us the Japanese doctor had removed his leg without any anaesthetic. We were both horrified, and the general ensured he be given special treatment.

The next day we were taken to the Ofuna Film Studio, where we spent a pleasant day filming Japanese movie stars, who had gone on producing films as their countrymen surrendered to the Allies.

After a few days of controlled public relations tours, the correspondents felt increasingly frustrated. Everyone was confined to Yokohama, but we wanted to get out to see the country for ourselves. We could not have our freedom until the official surrender.

Three days before the surrender, all the correspondents and some army officers were moved to the Dai-iti Hotel (later named the Dai-Ichi Hotel) in Tokyo. Opened in April 1938, the hotel, one of the largest in the Far East, had been built for the 1940 Summer Olympics, which Tokyo was meant to host. Those Olympics never took place. We were given our own room, which, although small, was a great luxury. There were no showers, so we all had to bathe in the tubs – even the short guys like me had their knees up under their chin. The taller warcos had to dangle their legs over the side of the bath. It would have been interesting to see the world's greatest athletes trying to have a bath, had the Games gone ahead.

On the evening before the formal surrender, the American cameramen and still photographers were called to a meeting at Radio Tokyo to discuss the camera positions on board the *Missouri*. The rest of us were not given the choice by the public relations officer, who had been sent out from the States for the job. The guy had not seen a shot fired during the war, but, for some reason, he had been put in charge. I asked him why we all couldn't choose our positions. 'None of you need to worry,' he said. 'They are all top spots. Besides, it's too late to make any changes.'

Boarding passes and camera positions were handed over and no questions were allowed. We were told we would be escorted to our position when we boarded the ship, and were warned if we tried to change our position, we would be thrown off. It was to be an all-American show. Other Allied forces had to stand off the *Missouri* until after the signing – they could only board the ship when everyone had left. Still, they were lucky just to see where it had all taken place.

On 2 September I awoke at 6 am to see the sun pouring in the window. The sky was perfectly clear, and there was no sign of rain. I got such a lovely feeling when I realised the conditions were perfect for such an historic event – I didn't want anything to spoil it. I felt incredibly lucky to be alive, after all the footslogging through the New Guinea jungle. I had seen so many young men killed. I was to board the biggest battleship in the world and send pictures of the surrender across the globe. Would I ever see the pictures? I began to think about home, wondering if I would get a job in Australia.

I pushed those thoughts aside and had a bath before meeting my friend, photographer Tom Shafer, in the dining room for breakfast. We packed the gear into the car, which was waiting outside the hotel, and drove to Yokohama to board the barge which would take us out to the *Missouri*, anchored in Tokyo Bay.

As we approached the ship, we could see it was packed from stem to stern with American troops. They filled every available position and even some spots in which you would never have thought anyone could fit. I worried there would be a fight over my camera position; these boys were obviously keen to see the deal done. I was escorted to my spot, where I only just squeezed in, with two hand-held cameras, each loaded with one hundred feet of 35 mm film and spares in the camera bag. There was no room for a tripod, so I had to hold the camera to film. I quickly surveyed the boat to determine how to shoot the major players. I was six feet above the table, about twenty feet from where MacArthur would be. He was to stand behind the table, directly facing the Emperor's nine representatives, who would sign the document. I was in a good position to catch the Japanese party as it appeared above the gangway, stepping onto the deck. I would be able to follow them, led by the new Foreign Minister, Mamoru Shigemitsu, as they walked across the deck to assume their positions. Shigemitsu, who had lost a leg to an assassin's bomb in 1932, used a walking stick to balance himself. I would see him hobble into position on his new artificial leg. I would also be able to see MacArthur, as he walked from his cabin to take up his position by the microphone and later sign the surrender documents for the Allies as a whole. I was pretty happy with my spot.

The Mighty Mo, as the *Missouri* was called, was surrounded by ships of all types, forming a spectacular picture in Tokyo Bay. It was the first time I had seen the mighty battleship, and what an awesome sight it was, decked out in flags, whose bright colours contrasted with a mass of khaki army uniforms filling every space and hanging from the yardarm. Anti-aircraft guns were fully manned and trained skyward, following rumours that Kamikaze pilots could attack the ship in a last-ditch effort to stop the surrender and save face for the Japanese nation.

The US Navy had a special camera stand built on the edge of the deck. What was about to be filmed looked like a complicated crowd scene in some big-budget Hollywood movie. Jammed together, all these men would have something to remember for the rest of their lives. Possibly they took the time to think about their buddies lying in cold graves on islands throughout the Pacific. I was certainly thinking about those dark days and how my luck had allowed me to come out of the war unscathed to capture such a magnificent picture on the *Missouri*.

There was just one small microphone to carry MacArthur's speech across the vast deck. Through the correspondents, the newly appointed Supreme Allied Commander would send his final wartime message to people around the world. Millions of people were listening to the events on radio, particularly in America, where it was early evening and families were eagerly awaiting the broadcast.

In the meantime, we were still waiting for the general to appear, and some of the crowd around me began jostling for the best vantage point. I was getting a little hot under the collar, and was concerned that I would not be able to operate the camera properly. I started jostling as well, until I finally lost my temper and threatened to bury my camera in the head of the first man who pushed me.

Australia lacked great representation. I was the only official Australian newsreel cameraman, and there was a still photographer, Arthur Bullard, working for the American Red Cross. We made up the Australian contingent, and we were only there because we were working for Americans. I had my American uniform on, so nobody would have even known I was Australian. There were no Australian troops on board representing the country and its wartime effort, but General Blamey stood there ready to sign the document. He was to have his moment in history, but, earlier, when MacArthur offered to have some Australians on board for the surrender, Blamey refused, unless he could bring a whole corps. As a result, the Australians had no ordinary soldiers representing them at the final moment of victory, which was an affront to those who had lost their lives and those who had survived the war.

Shortly before MacArthur appeared on deck, a Russian cameraman positioned himself next to Lieutenant General Derevyanko, who would sign the documents on behalf of the Soviet Union. The cameraman had not received permission from the general headquarters and we had all been threatened with removal if we left our designated positions. The US Navy police rushed in to grab the man but before they could act, General Derevyanko yelled, 'Leave him alone, don't touch him.' As if he were on fire, the navy police let go of the Russian, who was allowed to stay because the officials did not want to cause trouble just when events were getting under way. He got the best camera position on deck. The cameraman was not the only one in the Soviet delegation who did not follow orders. It was later reported that Fleet Admiral Chester W. Nimitz had to warn the whole Soviet delegation to stay in their positions or get off the ship.

As the Japanese dignitaries began filing on board to meet their conquerors, the humiliation showed on their faces. No one felt any pity for them. Toshikazu Kase, one of the Japanese delegation, reported that they were tortured by 'pillory'. 'A million eyes seemed to beat on us with the million shafts of a rattling storm of arrows barbed with fire,' he later wrote. Wearing a simple uniform and no decorations, MacArthur strode across the deck with his head held high. From behind a table, facing the Japanese delegates, he read the following speech:

Part II: War

We are gathered here, representatives of the major warring powers, to conclude a solemn agreement whereby peace may be restored. The issues, involving divergent ideals and ideologies, have been determined on the battlefields of the world and hence are not for our discussion or debate. Nor is it for us here to meet, representing as we do a majority of the peoples of the earth, in a spirit of destruction, malice, or hatred. But rather it is for us, both victors and vanquished, to rise to that high dignity which alone befits the sacred purposes we are about to serve, committing all of our people unreservedly to faithful compliance with the undertakings they are here formally to assume.

It is my earnest hope and indeed the hope of all mankind that from this solemn occasion a better world shall emerge out of the blood and carnage of the past – a world founded upon faith and understanding – a world dedicated to the dignity of man and the fulfillment of his most cherished wish – for freedom, tolerance, and justice.

The general moved over to the table, looked at Shigemitsu and directed him to sign the document. Shigemitsu signed and made room for General Yoshijiro Umezu, who signed on behalf of the Japanese Imperial General Headquarters. MacArthur sat down at 9.08 am to sign the document flanked by Percival and Wainwright. Representatives from the United States, China, the United Kingdom, the Soviet Union, Australia, Canada, France, the Netherlands and New Zealand added their signatures. Each representative was given a pen for his trouble. MacArthur added, 'Let us pray that peace be now restored to the world, and that God will preserve it always.'

After the signatures, MacArthur made a broadcast to the American people. He said, in part:

> Today, the guns are silent. A great tragedy has ended. A great victory has been won. The skies no longer rain death – the seas only bear commerce – men everywhere walk upright in the sunlight. The entire world is quietly at peace. The holy mission has been completed. And in reporting this to you, the people, I speak for the thousands of silent lips, forever stilled among the jungles and the beaches and in the deep water of the Pacific which marked the way. I speak for the unnamed brave millions homeward bound to take up the challenge of that future which they did so much to salvage from the brink of disaster.
>
> The energy of the Japanese race, if properly directed, will enable expansion vertically rather than horizontally. If the talents of the race are turned into constructive channels, the country can uplift itself from its present deplorable state into a position of dignity . . .

In his report, Kase said the general's speech transformed the deck into an altar of peace.

At that moment, the largest flight of American fighting aircraft ever formed flew low over Tokyo Bay and the Mighty Mo in one huge display. The noise was tremendous, matched only by the screams and cheers of the troops on board. It was the final nail in the Japanese coffin, a sight designed to impress the vanquished. I was overwhelmed at the opportunity to record such an historic event.

Tokyo, 1945. When the occupation forces moved in, children were found starving. In three months the Americans had won the hearts of the children. Photograph: US Signal Corps.

Mary Carty was Secretary for the US Catholic Women's League in Tokyo. These ladies raised thousands of dollars for charity, mostly for the Japanese who had no homes.

Part III

Occupation

Right: An interview with the Japanese prime minister in his private gardens. Below: Bill Carty in his den in Washington Heights with all his camera equipment. Photograph: Japanese Press.

Chapter Ten

Devastation

Yokohama, 1945. American sailors walk around the bombed area on the first day of the occupation of Japan.

SURRENDER MARKED A NEW PERIOD of freedom for all correspondents stationed in Japan. We were allowed to travel to any part of the country, and there were no arguments as to where to go – we headed straight for Hiroshima to film the aftermath of the first atomic bomb. Head office eagerly awaited footage of the site. No one knew much about the science of the bomb or its capabilities – it was the biggest story in the world.

I travelled with three others keen to film the damage. We left Yokohama by train and slept in the baggage car. When we

Flickers of History

finally arrived at Kyoto, after stopping at every station, we found the hotel staff courteous. The next day, we took a train, and then a taxi, to the devastated city.

Nothing during the war prepared us for the sight. Apart from a few buildings, the whole city had been flattened. Even the buildings that stood were empty shells. The rest formed a sea of rubble. The cab driver dropped us at the edge of the city and pointed out where the major buildings had been.

It was hard to know where to start filming. My camera rolled across the landscape, but I could not get high enough to take a wide shot of the city because there was nothing left to stand on. Three steps remained intact where the entrance to a bank had been. The stain on the steps, according to the cab driver, were the melted remains of a man who had been sitting there.

Most people had seen a blinding bluish-white flash that was 'brighter than a thousand suns'. Searing heat and crashes of thunder followed. Tens of thousands died instantly, burnt beyond recognition. This sad imprint was the most significant image for my camera – more potent than the rubble of the city. Today, the steps are preserved in a glass case in the Hiroshima Sanso Kinenkan War Memorial.

Hospital staff outside the bombsite worked tirelessly to treat the bomb victims. It was distressing to record graphic pictures of survivors covered in large blisters and burns. Many of the injured later died. We had no idea of the effects of radiation but, as far as I know, none of us suffered from spending time at the bombsite so soon after the blast.

I remain convinced that the bomb was the only way to end the war. More lives – some have estimated over one million –

would have been lost had the war dragged on and the Allies been forced to launch a full-scale invasion of Japan.

We stayed only one day in Hiroshima before returning to the Kyoto Hotel. When we checked out, I was presented with an enormous bill for the four of us. MacArthur was in the process of implementing regulations for occupation personnel to follow in Japan, so I told the manager that the supreme commander would take over every hotel in Kyoto the following week and he would take care of the bill. There was a lot of bowing, and then we left.

Coverage of Hiroshima was my first story after the surrender. With the war in Europe over in May 1945, Japan became the focal point. Paramount asked me to stay on for the newsreel pool to set up the Japan bureau, which was an indication of the increasing importance of worldwide news to the United States. Paramount applied to Washington for the necessary accreditation and once it was accepted, I was inducted into the Civilian American Force with the rank of a 'bird colonel', the equivalent of a full army colonel. I began the task of building a bureau that could give New York all the stories it required. I could move freely around Japan without permission from head office, and I was also responsible for China, Korea, Formosa (Taiwan), Hong Kong and the Philippines. I began by signing a contract with the Japan Nippon Newsreel Company to give me access to their coverage.

MacArthur had already given strict instructions to the Allied personnel under his command in Japan. The whole of Tokyo

Flickers of History

would be contained by general headquarters and MacArthur would live in that city and rule from the Dai Ichi Insurance Building. The rest of Japan was under the command of my friend, General Eichelberger, who was based in Yokohama. With control of the US Eighth Army, Eichelberger had command posts in villages and cities across the country.

Although some expressed concern about how they would react to being governed by a foreign power, the Japanese cooperated from the moment they surrendered. One of the first orders we received from MacArthur was 'no fraternising with the locals'. We were not allowed to feed the Japanese or give them money, and anyone who needed to employ a local needed authorisation from general headquarters, which would also take charge of all payment for work. We could not buy yen from the Japanese, and they could not use American dollars. Anyone caught breaking the rules could be deported immediately.

In February 1947, Colonel Edward Murray became the first Allied soldier caught breaking the rules. I had met him in Buna, New Guinea, where he commanded an American section and seemed to be a nice enough guy. Appointed custodian of the vaults in the Bank of Japan, he held a position of great trust, as the bank held all the loot stolen from various countries during the war – gold and silver bars, diamonds, gold plates and many other treasures. Although no one saw him take them, the colonel had helped himself to the buckets of diamonds.

Like other high-ranking soldiers, he was not searched when he travelled to and from the States. When he left Japan for the US to await reassignment, customs officials, who had been tipped off, found diamonds in his watch pocket. Hundreds more diamonds were found in a safe deposit box.

Forced to return to Japan after his arrest, Colonel Murray waited for his trial in Yokohama Jail. He held the dubious honour of being the first American brought to trial in Japan. This fact attracted every news outfit in the country.

I went down to the bank to take some pictures for the story. Accompanied by an armed guard, I saw the buckets of loot that would have surrounded him every day. I could not help but feel sorry for him as I watched him in court. He sat there with sagging shoulders looking dejected, staring at the saucers of diamonds of all sizes on the evidence table before him. Murray told officials that the diamonds, worth more than US$100 000, were 'legitimate souvenirs'. Wearing full military uniform and the medals he had earned during the war, the colonel had blown away thirty years of service. He was found guilty, sentenced to ten years in the federal penitentiary in Leavenworth, Kansas, and fined US$10 000. Eichelberger later reduced the sentence by two years because of the colonel's combat record.

Three months after the surrender, the US army told correspondents that the gravy train was over. We had to get out of army uniform and back into civilian clothes, and find our own accommodation and headquarters.

We found a clapped-out building in the centre of Tokyo. It had three storeys and an elevator, but it was in a filthy state, tucked away in an alley named Shimbun by the warcos – or 'newspaper alley'. The army agreed to supply and pay for the renovation by way of a loan, while the news organisations bought the building – it later became the Foreign Correspondents' Club. Japanese workers were brought in to scrub and paint, while bedrooms and showers were installed on the second floor. A new kitchen was built, with all the latest cooking stoves, and hospital cots, linen, blankets, pillows and other furniture were all supplied by the army. Food was also provided, and we arranged for Japanese help to cook. Liquor was available through the navy and no tax was ever paid. Army transportation was stopped and Paramount had to buy me a jeep. There were no more free rides.

We were allowed to set our own rules, within the larger regulations of the occupation. We could veto any new visitor or invite whomever we liked, except for the Japanese. But when Vincent Tubbs, the black American correspondent whom I had introduced to my family in Rose Bay in 1943, visited, there was trouble. He was sitting with a group of us when a US provost marshal spotted him through a window in the alley. He rushed in, singling out the only black man in a group of white men, and ordered him out of the club. 'No blacks are allowed in this club. Out.'

The correspondents immediately took umbrage, and I got on the phone to Eichelberger as the arguments ensued. He urged me to put the provost marshal on the phone, which I did. The general wasn't on the phone long. The marshal gave his name and number before putting the receiver down and walking out without a word to the warcos. I got back to the general to thank him, and he was pleased I had called: 'We can't let anything like this happen. He won't be doing anything like this again.' The club remained ours.

Part III: Occupation

So began the search for the best stories in Japan. The emperor featured high on the list, but MacArthur had issued strict instructions to the press not to bother the royal family, presumably so as not to upset the delicate political balance between the Allies and the Japanese. We still made many attempts to shoot stories on the emperor. In the meantime, there were plenty of other good yarns in Japan.

Locating missing American servicemen who may have been taken prisoner or died in Japan became a priority of the occupation forces. During the war, many flyers were shot down over Japan, and the survivors were usually kept in prison camps. Those lucky enough to make it to the end of the war told stories of the horror of their capitivity and of those who died from maltreatment. The dead were buried in a big pit in the Tokyo area, and army intelligence set out to find the mass grave. I had been invited to meet a team that was sent out to find such a grave, and arrived on the site just as a group of Japanese ex-soldiers started digging. Before long, they came across a number of bodies with ropes tied around their waists These were the remains of those executed. The smell from the grave was unbearable, so much so that the Japanese complained and stopped digging, but they were ordered to continue removing the bodies, which would be identified and shipped back to the US for proper burial.

Tokyo Rose was a well-known name to all who had served during the war. Behind the lines in New Guinea, commanding officers used to gather each afternoon to discuss the daily progress of battles. They used the time to listen to the war news produced by the Australian Broadcasting Corporation. At the same time, a Japanese propaganda program, 'Zero Hour', would be broadcast, using English speakers, such as Charles Cousens, a popular announcer with radio station 2GB in Sydney before he went to war and was captured by the Japanese. Whether or not Cousens was a willing or forced participant has never been fully resolved. He always claimed the broadcasts he prepared and presented were of little use to the Japanese, especially since he undermined the broadcasts by including information to assist the Allied cause and ridicule the enemy. Tokyo Rose, as she was dubbed by her listeners, was the most widely known announcer. She came on strong, urging the Australians to quit the war and save their lives. She even made up stories about the Americans based in Australia, trying to scare the Australian soldiers into thinking the Americans were running off with their wives. I heard her regularly during the Buna campaign. 'Americans are home with your wives,' she said. 'You fellas can do it, you can stop it.'

When the occupation began, a story circulated that a helpless young Japanese-American woman, Iva Toguri, had been stranded by the war and was one of three girls on radio. She had been forced to make broadcasts. At least, that was the story.

Those monitoring the broadcasts remained convinced that Toguri was the only woman involved. The American correspondents in Japan tried frantically to find her. US officials arrested her once but released her. I discovered she would be arrested a second time and got her address from intelligence officers.

Toguri lived in a two-room flat with her Portuguese husband on the outskirts of Tokyo. An officer told me when they would be picking her up, so I tried my luck the day before, on 16 October 1945. I knocked on her door and introduced myself before asking if she and her husband would be interested in an interview on camera. She refused outright to be interviewed with her husband, saying she would never allow him to be photographed, 'period'. I finally persuaded her to do the interview by reminding her of the coverage of Paramount News, which was widely known in prewar Japan.

She invited me in and introduced me to her husband. Iva told of her harassment by the press on her first arrest. I spent two hours in her home, getting a lot of good footage as she mapped out her life, from her childhood in California and graduation from the University of Los Angeles. Toguri told me she thought the Americans would enjoy her dance music and reminiscences about life back home, but then claimed circumstances had forced her to broadcast on a propaganda program. I left the interview on good terms.

The following day, I arrived at the same time as the military police, just as the arresting officer knocked on her front door. She must have been washing her hair because she answered the knock with her hair tied up in a towel. I stayed out of sight as the sergeant told her she was under arrest. He allowed her to finish drying her hair and collect a few personal things, before escorting her to the car. As they walked out, she caught sight of me with my camera rolling. Toguri was furious, hurling abuse at me as she realised she had been conned into doing the interview because of her impending arrest. It was a great story for me, and I felt no remorse, for I just thought of her damaging broadcasts. I never saw Tokyo Rose again, though I later learned she was charged with treason, fined US$10 000 and sent to prison. After serving six years of a ten-year sentence, she was released, and campaigned to clear her name. In 1977, she was pardoned by President Gerald Ford.

Chapter Eleven

War crimes

War Crimes Trial, Tokyo, 1948. Seven Japanese leaders were condemned to death, and sixteen others were sentenced to life imprisonment.

HIDEKI TOJO TOPPED THE LIST when, on 8 September 1945, MacArthur named Japanese leaders who would be tried as war criminals. As the man who initiated the war in the Pacific and directed Japan's war strategy until July 1944, General Tojo was viewed as evil by the western world. Correspondents redoubled their efforts to interview and photograph the man who would star in the war crimes trial.

There were a few old hands in Japan who knew Tojo's address, which was just outside Tokyo city. Given his notoriety,

Flickers of History

the correspondents took to hanging around his house, in case they scored an interview or a picture. On 11 September 1945, I was out of Tokyo on an assignment but two photographers, Chuck Garry of Associated Press and Charles Rosencrans of International News Service, and a correspondent, Russell Brines (author of *MacArthur's Japan*) headed out to Tojo's place. They joined a group who were outside the house, as the press was not allowed on the grounds. According to Garry, Tojo had chatted politely to the Japanese-speaking correspondents through an open window, although he would not give much away.

It was on that day that American agents arrived to arrest the general. According to historical accounts, (including Courtney Brown's *Tojo: The Last Banzai*) Tojo's wife said her husband was informed that he would be arrested by the agents. On hearing the information, Tojo closed the window and seconds later, a gun shot was heard. A former policeman and friend of the general's told Mrs Tojo that an MP kicked in the door of Tojo's study to discover him sprawled in a chair with a gun shot wound.

Tojo was treated at his house by US ambulance medics, while the director of the Ebara Hospital was summoned. A group which included some newsmen and arresting officers moved Tojo from the chair to a bed and covered him with a quilt. An American doctor, Captain Johnson, arrived soon after and administered a blood transfusion, (donated by an American) and a shot of morphine, before he was taken by ambulance to an American army hospital in Yokohama.

This remains the historical version of Tojo's suicide attempt but a number of correspondents told me a different account.

Garry, for instance, did not mention the arresting officers when he told me his story. He claimed that when they heard the gun shot, he and Rosencrans led the warcos inside the house and found Tojo lying in a pool of blood on the floor. Tojo had shot himself in the stomach and although he had missed his heart, the general was in danger of bleeding to death. The photographers, however, were not going to miss a chance for a good picture. Garry and Rosencrans hauled him into an armchair and Garry took some pictures. Knowing that his pictures would be splashed around the world, he never worried about hurting the number one war criminal. The photos took out a full page of *Life* magazine and brought in a cool US$500.

Garry could not tell me what happened after his photo session at the house – he raced off to his office to send the pictures to the US. However, Arthur Bullard, an Australian photographer who worked for the American Red Cross, told me that the ambulance medics took it upon themselves to stop off at the Dai-Ichi Hotel, to allow the remaining correspondents to get a decent picture of Tojo before he went to hospital. They flung open the ambulance doors for the correspondents, who had missed out on Garry's big break. There has been no mention of the medic's detour to the Dai-Ichi Hotel in the history books, perhaps because no one thought to record it or perhaps because it was shocking behaviour by today's standards. However, at the time, just a month after the war ended and with evidence of the Japanese atrocities still coming to light, there was no sympathy for Tojo, so his treatment shocked no one. Many believed a trial was not even necessary to hang the man considered most responsible for the Japanese war crimes. The thought that Tojo should be treated with the same dignity as a regular person did not even enter my head.

By the time I arrived at the hotel, the ambulance had just left so I raced over to the hospital, in time to see Tojo having a conversation with General Eichelberger through an interpreter. As I rolled the camera, Tojo presented Eichelberger with his sword, before he was taken to an operating theatre.

I waited at the hospital all night and in the morning it was announced that Tojo needed another blood transfusion. The best way to carry out the transfusion was to pump the blood directly from a donor into the arm of General Tojo. It was a long search but doctors finally found a US army sergeant who was willing to get involved in the bizarre operation to save the man whose soldiers were responsible for slaughtering thousands of Allied troops in the Pacific.

The donor lay in a hospital cot set up alongside Tojo's bed but the doctor had trouble finding the donor's vein. By the time he got the needle in the right spot, the sergeant's screams could be heard throughout the hospital. The link was made to Tojo's arm and then we all watched, with camera's rolling, as American blood flowed into the veins of Japan's most infamous war criminal.

Tojo's spectacularly unsuccessful suicide attempt disappointed many Japanese soldiers and civilians who remembered the general's orders to commit harakiri rather than surrender to the enemy. When the time came for his own arrest, Tojo's conviction proved to be lacking.

When Tojo recovered, he was sent to a prison on Omori, a small island in Tokyo Bay, between Tokyo and Yokohama.

There he waited with many other Japanese generals, admirals, commanders and politicians for the trials to begin. Eichelberger gave me exclusive access to the prisoners on Omori before they were transferred on 8 December 1945 to Sugamo prison in Tokyo, where there would be no chance of getting pictures before the trial.

The main trial of high-ranking (Class A) war criminals took place in Tokyo in the former war ministry buildings. Those on trial included: two ex-prime ministers, Tojo and Koki Hirota; the former war minister Seishiro Itagaki; former war vice minister Heitaro Kimura; the ex-chief of the naval affairs bureau, Takasumi Oka; and two ex-generals, Kenji Doihara and Iwane Matsui. Three of the twenty-eight in this top category never faced trial: Yosuke Matsuoka, an ex-civilian foreign minister, and ex-admiral Osami Nagano died while awaiting trial; and the third, Shumei Okawa, was deemed mentally unfit to face the court.

An international tribunal of eleven judges from the United States, the Soviet Union, China, the United Kingdom, Canada, France, the Netherlands, New Zealand, India, the Philippines and Australia presided over the trial. MacArthur appointed an Australian judge, Sir William Flood Webb, as president of the tribunal. Having served on the Supreme Court of Queensland for over twenty years, Sir William became that State's Chief Justice in 1940, a position he held until 1946. From that year, until his retirement in 1958, he was a justice of the High Court. Sir William, who had acted as a war crimes commissioner, attracted MacArthur's attention after the general read a special report investigating Japanese war crimes in places where Australians had fought, including Papua and New Guinea. MacArthur sent a plane to Brisbane to fly Sir William and his personal staff to Tokyo, where they would stay at the city's best hotel, the Imperial – one of the few to escape the Allied bombing.

I felt proud that an Australian had been chosen for the top job, and arranged to meet Sir William on his arrival. His appointment was big news in America, where the public awaited the start of the war trials with anticipation. This was the man who would exercise a great influence over whether the criminals would hang or remain in prison for the rest of their lives.

Sir William was an impressive man, and not just because of his position. I would not have been surprised had he been haughty and difficult, especially with the press, but he was not. In private, he was quietly spoken with a natural charm and friendliness, endearing him to all. I invited him to dinner at the Foreign Correspondents' Club and, much to the delight of my colleagues, he accepted immediately. We knew we would have no trouble getting information during the war trials.

Opening statements were given on 3 May 1946, and the trial began on 3 June. We were told it would be over in three months, but it lasted two years and ninety-eight days. Hundreds of witnesses were called, and affidavits came from hundreds more. The main trial was both sensational and tedious. Given the number of defendants, there was an enormous amount of evidence to absorb, in the form of transcripts, footage and photographs. Lawyers went through the evidence in minute detail and, as a consequence, the trial seemed to stretch on forever. At times the trial captured world attention, as individuals struggled to understand how human beings could treat each other with such barbarity; at other times, the proceedings bordered on the comic.

Before the lunch adjournment on the first day, Sir William halted the proceedings to allow film cameramen and still photographers onto the floor of the court to shoot close-ups of the defendants. The still boys raced in, took their pictures and then took off. I held back until they had finished to take clear footage. I began moving along the line of defendants, to get close-ups of each man. Tojo sat in the front row, but, when I trained my camera on him, I noticed the guy behind, Shumei Okawa, muttering and fidgeting. I immediately rolled the camera. Suddenly Okawa leaned forward and gave Tojo a mighty whack on the top of his bald head. A shocked Tojo turned to find out what was happening, then looked towards the camera with a half-smile on his face. I got the whole thing on film, and there was not another cameraman or photographer on the floor of the court. The film made a still in *Time* magazine and five newsreels. US military police escorted Okawa from the courtroom and took him to a hospital for psychiatric evaluation. He was declared unfit to defend himself, and sent to a mental hospital, where he stayed until 1949 before being discharged. Okawa died of a heart attack nine years later.

On 12 November 1948, the tribunal handed down its judgment. The Allied and the Japanese press had been informed that there would be a decision. With all our lights and camera stands, the courtroom could have been a

Hollywood set. I grabbed a position that gave me a clear view of both the prisoners and the judges.

The call came for the court to stand and the participants and the audience rose to their feet while the judges moved into their chairs. The prisoners were marched into the dock, where they arose one by one to hear their sentence. They were the seven most senior prisoners: Tojo, Hirota, Itagaki, Doihara, Kimura, and ex-generals Muto and Matsui. Most had no idea of what their fate would be. All were found guilty and sentenced to death. Of the other Class A criminals, sixteen were sentenced to life imprisonment, while two others were given prison terms of twenty and seven years respectively. Tojo appeared shocked by the final verdict. He looked up towards the public gallery where his wife had sat for the whole of the trial and bowed to her. She returned the bow. Tojo later wrote in his prison diary, 'There is nothing strange about the sentence passed on me. I expected to be put to death, by hanging. But the sentences on the others surprised me.'

Although the Allied powers had already decided not to prosecute the emperor before the trial began, Sir William Webb told me that he believed Hirohito had to bear the responsibility for Japan's wartime efforts. This much was evident in his announcement of the formal judgment, when he offered his own opinion. Sir William told the court that while evidence showed the emperor did not want war, his authority for Japan's involvement was required and as leader, Hirohito should have withheld his imprimatur, whether or not his personal safety was threatened by such a decision. Sir William also wrote that he was not suggesting the emperor should have been prosecuted, as his immunity was 'in the best interests of all the Allied Powers'.

This last point, however, did not square with my private conversations with Sir William, who subsequently became godfather to my daughter, Patricia. During his many visits to my home, Sir William told me that he had called on MacArthur before the trial to discuss the position of the emperor. If Tojo was guilty, then so was Hirohito, Sir William had said. MacArthur was adamant that the emperor could not be tried and hanged because it would demoralise the Japanese people and cause more trouble than good. From our conversations, I was led to believe that the issue caused quite a deep rift in the relationship between Sir William and MacArthur. Perhaps, in his final judgment, Sir William had to present the Allied position, quite apart from his true personal views.

Tojo and the six others were bustled out of court and taken back to Sugamo. It was the last time the prisoners were seen by the public. They were told they would be hanged on Thursday, 24 December at one minute past midnight.

Each of the men spent their last day writing letters and speaking with the Buddhist priest, Dr Shinsho Hanayama, prison chaplain at Sugamo. As a spokesman for the condemned, Tojo asked for their last meal to be Japanese. He wrote a final poem to the world:

> Farewell to all,
> For today I cross the earthly mountains
> And gladly go
> To the folds of Buddha.

Sheishiro Itagaki wrote:

> Humbly do I kneel
> In front of our great God
> And beg forgiveness
> For all my sins.

Koki Hirota did not leave a poem but said he hoped Japan would soon be able to join the international family and contribute its part to permanent world peace. His wish has come true.

At MacArthur's request, a small party gathered to witness the execution just after midnight on the appointed date. There were doctors and prison personnel, as well as William J. Sebald, MacArthur's political adviser, General Shang Chen, representative of China, Patrick Shaw, representative of Australia, Lieutenant General Derevyanko, representative of the Soviet Union, and Captain Walter Pennino of the US Army.

Pennino, a friend of mine, later described the executions. To ensure he was not followed by the press, the army used three different cars to take him to Sugamo prison. Four of the condemned men – Doihara, Matsui, Tojo, and Muto – walked to the gallows in a makeshift chapel, muttering Buddhist prayers. They took the thirteen steps up to the gallows platform, where each stood in his allotted position. Black hoods were placed over their heads, the ropes adjusted and the trap doors released. Within minutes the four were pronounced dead. The remaining three criminals went through the same process. No photographs of the executions exist. MacArthur told Sebald that they 'would violate all sense of decency'.

Their bodies were carried away in wooden coffins in an army truck for cremation in a bombed-out crematorium in Yokohama. The press desperately tried to find the location, but the US Army had cremated the bodies in great secrecy by the following morning. Seven rusty old ovens were fired up to end the war crimes trial.

Chapter Twelve

The emperor

The emperor and his family at their summer residence south of Yokohama. Photograph: Eighth Army photographer.

AUSTRALIAN PEOPLE are generally a relaxed lot. We're a little bit rowdy, perhaps. We definitely have a healthy scepticism of authority. I had difficulty understanding the Japanese way. They were reared with such strict discipline at home and at school.

Among our first orders from MacArthur was no fraternising or feeding the Japanese. Many were starving and begged the Allied personnel for food. The children soon learned that many of the foreigners carried sweets with them and flocked around us in the street. At our Foreign Correspondents' Club, the Japanese domestic help could not eat from the kitchen, so all the slops from the table went into a GI can and the Japanese took their food from that.

In my daily work I got to know many Japanese and met them in different situations. I visited schools, where the teacher just had to say 'quiet', and there was not one whisper. At train stations, the staff obeyed the stationmaster's orders with enthusiasm. Train passengers travelled according to the conductor's rules. Perhaps this explains why MacArthur never had any trouble once the Japanese government surrendered to his command – as the new authority, he had to be obeyed.

The emperor, though, was always the central authority figure to the Japanese. Although his power had been neutralised by the Americans, the Japanese worshipped him. Before the war, if he visited cities, the crowds on the street turned their backs to bow because they were not allowed to gaze on the face of the so-called Son of Heaven. For an Australian, it seemed ridiculous to show your respect by turning your back.

The occupation chipped away at much of the emperor's mystique. In late September 1945, MacArthur arranged a meeting with Hirohito at the general's home in the former US embassy. The press were not allowed in, so we had to satisfy ourselves with pictures of the emperor's car. But it seemed from that moment of contact, signs began to appear that the emperor would shed some of the strictly formal rules that had applied in prewar Japan.

Head office welcomed any footage on Hirohito. International audiences were hungry to learn more about Japan's remote royal

Part III: Occupation

family. I prevailed on the First Cavalry Division to lend me a Piper Cub to provide my first footage of the buildings that made up the Imperial Palace grounds, including the spot where a bomb was dropped during one of the Tokyo raids.

We needed permission from the emperor's secretary to enter the gates, for he was not only protected by his own special police, who guarded the palace, but also by American soldiers with fixed bayonets, standing watch around the clock.

In the beginning of the occupation, we were given false information on the emperor's movements. Once we were tipped off of his arrival at Tokyo railway station. The whole press contingent lined up there for two hours before finally giving it away.

At that time, I shared a room at the club with Tom Shafer, a still photographer for United Press pictures. I had met Tom a few years before on the American base in New Guinea, when he was taking shots of an enterprising GI who had set up a barber shop with a steam bath. It was a popular spot for the officers and men, so I did a story for DOI, before we both had a haircut and a bath.

One morning in the club, Tom woke me up and asked if I would like a story on the emperor. I jumped at the opportunity, and pressed for details, but Tom would tell me nothing more. We took off in the Paramount jeep and met up with Tom's boss, 'Peg' Vaughan, a bureau chief for United Press. He took us to the Tamagorio mausoleum in Tokyo's western suburbs, the shrine for the emperor's ancestors. Hirohito planned to tell his deceased relatives that Japan had lost the war. It was to be an extremely symbolic moment, and we were under strict instructions not to get any closer than twenty feet or harass the emperor in any way.

Hirohito was driven to the bottom of the steps leading up to the tomb. We both moved in to take shots of the emperor getting out of the car and moving up the stairs. When we tried to follow, his secretary stood in front of us, blocking the way. The emperor then turned to look at us and we trained our cameras on him, before he continued up the stairs. Shafer, a big man with a large stomach, tried again to get up the stairs. When the secretary jumped in front of him, he pushed him with his substantial gut. The secretary threatened to call in the security guards, and we backed off. I remembered MacArthur's orders and knew we would be in serious trouble if we did not follow them.

The emperor stayed in the tomb for about thirty minutes before descending the stairs and stopping at the bottom. He seemed to be giving us a chance for more photographs because he looked straight at the cameras.

Once the emperor left, the secretary allowed us to run up the stairs to see what it was all about. In front of the tomb stood a long table, covered in a white tablecloth, with offerings of rice, fruit and cooked chicken. Hirohito offered the food as a part of his worship. Even without film of him making the offering, the office was pleased to have some footage of the emperor. I had Peg to thank for letting me in on it. Peg was an old hand in Japan, having lived there before the war. An avid duck hunter, he was found dead in Tokyo Bay later in the occupation after he went out shooting by himself on his day off. There was speculation of foul play, but the post-mortem was never released. It was a sad end for the experienced writer.

Part III: Occupation

Although the Americans were the victors, MacArthur treated Hirohito with respect. But, at the same time, the Americans wanted to show off their own culture. They organised a rodeo and air circus on Armistice Day in the first year of the occupation. The star attraction, so the organiser told me at the Foreign Correspondents' Club, was one of the emperor's horses, White Frost. I figured, if I couldn't get much of the emperor on film, I would surely get one of his horses. The organiser, Lieutenant Dick Ryan, offered me some exclusive shots of the royal horse before the show. He even let me jump in the saddle for a picture.

Ryan put the beautiful white horse through his tricks for my cameras, and then went on to perform before the crowd. He told the crowd of American personnel and Japanese families at the Meiji Shrine Stadium that White Frost was the emperor's horse. The locals were stunned at the sight of an American sitting on the emperor's horse. Not to be outdone, Major General William Chase, who had taken his First Cavalry Division right through the Pacific, rode General Tojo's horse around the stadium.

The Japanese had been issued an open invitation to the first ever rodeo staged in that country. It marked a real breakthrough for the occupation forces, as they won great admiration from the Japanese for putting on the show. Head office loved the footage, which it showed around the world. Some months later I discovered I had been diddled. Ryan had substituted a racehorse for the emperor's horse. It seems the lieutenant was just a good salesman. The last I heard was that he headed back to the US with the phony White Frost in tow.

The first time Hirohito walked among his people after the official surrender, there could have been a riot. He went public in Osaka and Kobe, and ordinary Japanese citizens were given the chance not only to look at him, but to get close enough to touch him. In the old regime, they would have lost their heads for such an impertinent act. The noise was unbelievable as the people waved flags and cheered him on.

For the police, it was a nightmare to control. They could not have stopped an attack on the emperor in such a frenzy. There was no bowing this time – the emperor was swamped.

I organised a jeep with two others, Father Patrick O'Connor, a former war correspondent representing the Irish papers, and Carl Mydans, who worked for *Time* and *Life* magazines. Carl and I were in and out of the jeep all afternoon, producing wonderful shots that got worldwide release.

The emperor made more and more appearances in public. Tokyo station was cleared once when Hirohito wanted to take a ride on a train. After the station was swept and sprayed with water, a red carpet was laid on the dried surface for the emperor's forty-yard walk from his car to the carriage. The emperor had a personal train that he had used until the occupation. If he went out in it, other trains were cleared ahead of it. After the surrender, Eichelberger commandeered the train for his inspection tours around the country.

A department store was the next target for the emperor. We couldn't believe it when we were informed he would take a walk through a store on the Ginza for the first time. On this occasion, he brought the empress. I could not imagine what he was thinking. I couldn't work out whether he was just curious, or if he felt he had to do it. The excited employees couldn't believe he had chosen their store. A sea of security guards

Part III: Occupation

stood on duty inside and another contingent of Japanese police stood outside. Japanese cameramen had lit the sections he planned to visit, so we all had plenty of light. The press were allowed in a small section, roped off from the royal personage.

As soon as the emperor and his wife arrived, all decorum disappeared. No ropes could stop the press from surging forward in one body, lunging for the best shot. I became entangled with the scribblers and photographers in the front row. With a lot of pushing and shoving, I kept the camera viewfinder glued to my eye. At one stage, I stood about three feet from the emperor, at eye level, before the head security guard gave me a few hefty shoves back. My camera left my face long enough to tell him to keep his hands off me.

Before long the emperor began agreeing to open up the palaces for occasional publicity. General Eichelberger gave me permission to photograph the emperor's trained falcons at one of the imperial palaces south of Yokohama. It was an exclusive picture story. Japanese keepers trained and cared for the falcons, which were used to entertain the emperor's guests. The keeper's arms were padded to protect them from the claws, and each falcon had a long rope attached to its leg, so it had a limited circuit.

Wild ducks were kept in wicker baskets and, before the show, the birds were prepared for their deaths. The keeper took one duck out at a time, plucked a feather and poked the quill in its eyes. The keeper explained that, when released, a blinded duck instinctively flies straight up into the sky. When released the falcon immediately flew up to kill the duck. It was a great show, though the visitors were not told of the birds' handicap. The ducks were then cooked for dinner.

Flickers of History

My good standing with the First Cavalry Division helped me get into the summer palace in Hayama. Men from the division were posted to protect the emperor and his family, but they tipped me off about his vacation and arranged for me to get inside to photograph the first intimate pictures of the emperor and his family for world audiences. Everyone was very polite and there was a great deal of bowing, but no conversation. The newsreels trumpeted the pictures widely:

<u>UNIVERSAL NEWSREEL
COVERS WORLDWIDE EVENTS</u>

MIKADO AS A FAMILY MAN
Hayama, Japan – In these intimate pictures of the Jap Emperor and his royal family, you will see them together for the first time as they pose for cameramen in the villa south of Tokyo.

Once the emperor became more conversant with the occupation, he began allowing his son, Crown Prince Akihito, to meet some of the new inhabitants. I was permitted to take pictures of the ten-year-old boy visiting his father's private museum for the first time.

General headquarters decided to have a horseshow and invite some Japanese children, including the emperor's. It formed part of MacArthur's plan to democratise the Japanese and to expose them to the American lifestyle. The crown prince and two of his sisters, Princesses Kazuko and Atsuko, sat in the public stand with other children, who were oblivious to the royal presence. Their bodyguards were inconspicuous. By that stage, my family had joined me to live in Japan and my son Jim and an American boy, Michael Evans, tried to talk to him. They did not know who he was. Akihito was shy and unaccustomed to mixing with foreign boys his own age. Not only that, he could not speak any English, so they soon gave up.

My wife, Mary, worked that day on a hot dog stand for the US Catholic Women's League to raise money for charity. The Japanese children had taken to the American food with great enthusiasm, so I decided to try the crown prince. He had never even seen a hot dog before, let alone tasted one. I asked Mary to make up some hot dogs with all the trimmings and present them to the royal family. She was too shy to give it to them on camera, so I gave it to them as I rolled the camera. It provided some great pictures for me, with the prince's expression telling the whole story. In a matter of seconds, every photographer in the joint had sniffed out the story, surrounding the young boy with cameras. My exclusive had gone out the window.

The increasing contact with the outside world probably convinced the emperor that his son should learn English. He offered the position of tutor to an American Quaker and author of children's books, Elizabeth Vining. MacArthur gave his permission for her to take up the position, and she swapped a quiet existence in Pennsylvania for a royal life in Japan.

My family and I were living in Washington Heights when she arrived in October 1946. She began teaching the twelve-year-old prince and a number of other Japanese boys in his class. In the meantime, my children were sent to the Sacre Coeur School in Tokyo, but most of the American or foreign children were sent to the American elementary school, which was well equipped. The school's bus picked up children at their front doors from all over Tokyo. All the teachers were American, and, to me, the teaching methods appeared casual, although there was some discipline. Following the increasing public appearances of the crown prince, the school sent him an invitation to see how an American school operated.

Elizabeth thought it was a wonderful idea and received permission from the imperial household. She decided to give the crown prince a lesson in democracy before he visited the school. On the blackboard she wrote words, such as representative, nominate, vote, elect and ballot. The class had to vote for the boys who would accompany the prince on his visit. She demonstrated how to vote and wrote the list of candidates, based on their knowledge of English, on the blackboard. Akihito nominated a boy, but his English was not good enough, so he refused.

The winning candidates met Elizabeth and her assistant, Tané, at Harajuku Station in Tokyo at 9 am. They were joined by the prince and a group of officials who would also visit the school. The idea was to keep the visit a secret, but, like all official secrets, word soon leaked out. The three-car convoy was met by Japanese lining the streets, bowing and waving as it passed by. The Japanese press got word of the visit, but the foreign correspondents were left in the dark. I came out just as the convoy passed my front door, heading up to the Washington Heights school. I recognised the car and ran to my own jeep, which had all my gear on board. I passed the cars and arrived at the school in time to catch the party getting out of their own cars – just as if I had known all along. Elizabeth later wrote a book, *Windows for the Crown Prince* (1952), which detailed her life in Japan, and she recounted the school visit and my lucky find. She wrote:

> Bill Carty of Paramount News just happened to come out of his house at the moment when the three cars passed. A very quick-witted young man, he took in the situation at a glance, and I have never seen anyone move faster.

Akihito was so unaccustomed to being with foreign boys that the pictures said it all. His interaction with the children was like a microcosm of what was happening in the major Japanese cities during the occupation. The country had been closed to foreigners for so long that it took some effort to understand foreign habits and cultures. Akihito was simply learning what his countrymen were learning. The most striking image of the day was the most simple – the crown prince sitting next to an American child.

My first impression of Elizabeth was that she was cold and unfriendly. She considered my pictures an invasion of her own and the young prince's privacy. But, as time went by, we became good friends and eventually she got used to the camera. Originally on a two-year contract, Elizabeth ended up staying four years – Elizabeth had charmed the emperor and his family and MacArthur. At the end of her stay, she received the Third Order of the Sacred Crown, a rare order, from the Japanese government.

Chapter Thirteen

Family business

At the foot of Mount Fuji, Bill, Mary, Pauline, Helen and James pose above the frozen Lake Yamanaka. Photograph: US Signal Corp.

IT WAS MORE THAN A YEAR before my family joined me in Japan. When asked to cover the occupation, I didn't believe it was safe enough to bring them to Japan. For a long time, it was not even seen as a possibility. General Eichelberger put the idea into my head. Since the start of the occupation we had had a weekly lunch appointment. He asked me at one of these meetings why I didn't bring them up. I had not seen my family for eighteen months, so it didn't worry me when head office refused to pay for their journey from Sydney to Tokyo – I was more than happy to pay. I took a month off to return to Australia to organise their trip.

My transport – a RAAF DC-3 – was extremely uncomfortable. My backside was sore after seven days in a bucket seat, island-hopping through the Pacific. As an armed forces plane, it was a regulation ride all the way: parachutes worn at all times, army rations, and not an attendant in sight. At Darwin, there were no planes scheduled to fly south, so I prepared for a long wait. Luckily, a four-engine American troop carrier came to my rescue and the words Paramount News got me on board for the trip to Brisbane, via Townsville. That night as we stopped in the north Queensland town, I was starving, but could buy nothing other than a pint of milk. It was the first milk I had seen in months.

The plane carried a load of Australians who had been working for the Americans in the Philippines. They had filled their baggage with American cigarettes and tobacco, and the customs officers looked at their luggage with interest. Australians had to pay tax on all of those sorts of items, so each man was presented with a hefty bill. No one could afford to pay, so the cigarettes were confiscated. My own luggage was packed with gifts for the family, as well as cigarettes, so I was wondering what my own bill would be. The officer took one look at my American uniform and said, 'We don't really need to see you.' They didn't charge the yanks, so I was clear. I offered him a carton of cigarettes, which he readily accepted and stashed behind a door.

My family took the overnight train to meet me in Brisbane. It was a hell of a trip, one which I had to do on the way back to Sydney. There were no sleeping cars, just an old boxcar that carried ten people sitting knee to knee. It had a toilet and a basin at one end, so if someone wanted to use it, the passenger in the window seat had to stand and lift the seat for the person to get into the cubicle. With ten-year-old Helen, seven-year-old Jim and four-year-old Pauline, who had to be nursed, the trip was a nightmare. For me, it was a wonderful reunion at one of Brisbane's best hotels, and the train ride back was incidental.

I made the arrangements for their travel, including passports and vaccinations, and booked them on an American freighter that would sail for Japan in a matter of weeks. After a fortnight at home, I travelled back to Tokyo – another seven-day journey. On arrival, I flew into a rage when I saw the awaiting telegram. Mary had cabled to say the ship had been diverted to the Philippines and she could not come as planned. The Australian armed forces in charge of the ships travelling to Japan had refused permission because she was going to an American base in Tokyo instead of the Australian base at Kure.

I went straight to MacArthur's headquarters for help, and, within a week, she was leaving on the *Taiping*, and arriving at Kure, on Honshu. I would not get to see my family for Christmas, but it was a relief to know they were on their way.

As I made preparations for their arrival, Mary was having a difficult time on board the *Taiping*. They had been booked into a four-berth cabin above deck with a porthole. Meanwhile, an Australian politician and his family made a late booking for Japan. Mary and the children were moved into a three-berth cabin below deck with no porthole. Mary had to sleep on the floor so the three children had beds, and the four of them spent eighteen stuffy days in the bowels of the boat.

Flickers of History

Mary must have wondered what she was doing. From the moment I rang to tell them to come to Japan, life had been a roller-coaster for her. While she didn't tell me at the time, some people had been nasty about our decision to go to Japan. 'How can you go to a country like that after the way the Japanese treated our prisoners?' people asked. Others said, 'Surely you wouldn't take young children to a country full of savages.' Mary had never been overseas before, she just had to trust me that the decision was right. In fact, she had been making plans to build a house in Sydney's northern suburbs. My call had put a stop to all of that – a decision I later regretted.

The family arrived at Kure, washed-out but relieved, and we took an overnight train to Tokyo. We planned to live in a new development called Washington Heights, but it was not quite finished, so I had arranged temporary accommodation in a new building called Jefferson Heights.

On her second day in Japan, Mary, whose head was still spinning from the trip, attended her first official function and was guest of honour at a lunch given by the Eichelbergers. The general had a beautiful western-style house on top of a bluff in Yokohama. He loved to entertain, and the correspondents were his favourite people, especially those few who were in New Guinea with him.

We were busy organising the ordinary aspects of life, which, in a normal situation, would have been mundane. While we waited for the house to be built, I applied for a car. The US Army had brought in brand new cars for their occupation personnel to buy using a lottery system. You had to fill in a form and, each week, a winner was drawn. The winner paid a

Part III: Occupation

set price for the car, free of tax, then the army registered it, attached the number plate, and you drove it away. I filled in the form and, within a week, I owned a brand new Ford. Mary needed a car to take the family around, so I taught her how to drive in my jeep. While she preferred the jeep because it was smaller and easier to handle, she had to make do with the latest model Ford instead.

Two weeks later, we moved into Washington Heights. To accommodate the large occupation force, the US Army took over and refurbished the best houses untouched by the bombing in Tokyo and Yokohama, and compensated the owners. Japanese were employed to build the new housing developments, most of which were named after American generals. Washington Heights contained one thousand two- and three-bedroom homes built for officers between the ranks of captain and full colonel in the Civilian American Forces.

My rank was equivalent to a full colonel, so I took a three-bedroom home with all the modern conveniences. It was fully furnished, with gas heating in the floor. For this house, we paid the princely sum of $8.00 per month. The area also had everything a modern community needed – a chapel for all religions, a doctor's surgery and a chemist, as well as a lot of party facilities, including a large ballroom, small rooms for private parties, several bars and a kitchen. We bought our food from a PX (an army supply shop) and commissary, which was stacked with fresh and frozen vegetables and meat flown in from the US. The Americans took over a department store on Ginza, stocking it full of American clothing and merchandise for their personnel to buy tax-free. A team of Japanese gardeners maintained the grounds. If that were not enough, there was a hotline provided to all the residents just in case of a domestic disaster. An army unit stayed on to do those urgent jobs around the area, with each job supervised by an army sergeant.

When Mary became pregnant with our fourth child, I applied for a larger house. With four children, we were entitled to a five-bedroom Japanese house. My request was approved. A large wall framed an expansive garden. The house came with five Japanese servants and a gardener, as well as an amah to look after the new baby. Mary supervised the cooking, as the Japanese were unused to preparing western food. We rarely ate Japanese food.

There was only one problem with the new house – rats. Tokyo had been plagued by rats ever since the Allied bombing towards the end of the war. Special rat units had been sent out to rid the houses of the creatures. When we moved in, our place had been fastidiously cleaned and the furniture was new. We couldn't find a fault, but, after a couple of weeks, we noticed a strange odour that we couldn't identify. The birth of a baby girl, Patricia Ann, diverted our attention. One night, shortly after she was brought home, our baby was bitten on the finger by a rat. After one phone call, a team of ratters arrived and tracked down the smell to our bedroom. There they found a nest with two dead rats in it in our bedpost. The Japanese workers did a great job cleaning the place out and we were rat free for the rest of our stay.

Born in the US hospital, Patricia automatically became an American citizen. She was baptised by the Apostolic delegate, Archbishop Paul Marella, assisted by US chaplain, Father Brooker, and Sir William and Lady Webb were her godparents.

Part III: Occupation

Babies invite attention everywhere, but little blonde Patricia attracted more than her fair share in Japan, where she was regarded not only with curiosity but affection. Her Japanese amah, Kikeo, sang and spoke to her in Japanese from the time she was born and Patricia responded with delight. Once she was sitting in the back of our car with Mary when we were stopped at traffic lights on Ginza. An elderly man, who was waiting to cross the road, smiled at Patricia, who was staring straight back at him. She responded immediately with a smile and bowed twice. The man could hardly believe his eyes and he quickly bowed three times before I drove off, unaware of the show in the back seat. When told about it later, I couldn't help but think of what a wonderful shot it would have made to show the new relationship between Japan and the rest of the world.

Our household was always full of people, and we kept a spare room for visitors, many of whom were priests. During the occupation, all visitors to Tokyo needed a special pass, but many of our guests did not obtain permission. I didn't have the heart to turn away people who needed a bed, so we broke the rules. Once the clergy heard of our hospitality, most visiting priests dropped in to stay or pay a visit at least once on their trips to Japan.

One such visitor was Father Jim Bell, the Provincial of the Australia Province of the Marist Fathers. Father Bell arrived in Japan in 1948 to carry out a feasibility study for establishing a new mission, on the urging of Father Lionel 'Sam' Marsden, who had spent the war as a Catholic chaplain and prisoner of the Japanese in the infamous Changi prison and on the Burma Railway. Father Bell was completely unaware of the strict rules for foreign visitors entering Tokyo but found our front gate in the Tokyo suburb of Ebisu, named after the God of Good Fortune.

We arrived home from a shopping trip to find a strange priest waiting outside our gate. When he told us his story, we welcomed him with open arms, providing food, transportation and a room. Father Bell had never lived with a family during his time in the priesthood so he was enthralled with the experience of sitting down to dinner with three talkative children and a baby girl every night. Every morning he said mass in the living room, using our son Jim and sometimes Mary and Helen, to assist on the altar.

After travelling outside Tokyo, Father Bell decided on Nara as the best location for a mission and returned to Australia full of enthusiasm. He appointed Sam Marsden as superior of the new mission and the former POW arrived on our doorstep in 1949.

Like all POWs in Changi and along the Burma Railway, Father Marsden suffered at the hands of the Japanese. On one occasion, he was badly beaten when he asked for food for a sick prisoner. Understandably, those who suffered so much at the hands of the Japanese were filled with hatred for them but Father Marsden, while still a prisoner, had made a promise that if he survived the war, he would go to Japan to teach the gospel of forgiveness and compassion.

We were honoured to think that he would choose our home to revisit his captors. The work that these priests carried out revealed to us how tolerance and love can be shown to a former enemy. Australians and other Allied countries still held deep hatred for the Japanese, and, before we went to Japan, we felt the same way. The visiting priests showed us that the

Part III: Occupation

Japanese were as human as anybody else. Jim later told us that the influx of priests through the house and the knowledge of their work influenced his decision to become a priest.

The arrival of my family signalled the start of a sociable period for me. Having families around meant less talk about work among the correspondents and staff and the forming of more lasting friendships. Party season seemed to extend throughout the year. Many of the parties were held by the embassies, and many of the VIPs on the official invitation lists were ambassadors and army officers. Viscount Montgomery of Alamein, who commanded the British victories over the Germans in North Africa, Major General Bill Chase, who was in charge of the Bank of Japan, and Reverend Edmund A. Walsh, a Regent of the Foreign Service from the US, swirled past us at various functions.

WVTR was the key station in the Armed Forces Radio Network in the Far East command. It broadcast out of the same studios as had Tokyo Rose and Charles Cousens during the war. The station hosted a fifth anniversary party for the service. All of the press and big brass in Tokyo made the invitation list.

With the radio playing in the background, we prepared to go to the party. Suddenly the announcer warned people to stay in their houses, for there was a disturbance in the Bay of Tokyo and no one was sure what was happening. I ran around the house, grabbing my gear. I heard that a huge monster had just shown its head in the bay near Yokohama. By this stage the kids were screaming, 'Daddy, don't go.' They were frightened out of their wits, terrified something might happen to me. Mary pleaded with me to stay behind. Just as I opened the door to leave, the announcer called, 'There goes the Paramount News cameraman out to photograph the monster.' It was obviously a hoax. 'Surprise, surprise, all is well. Nothing is happening in the Bay of Tokyo. It's the station's fifth anniversary.'

Once the children had settled down, we left them with the Japanese servants and headed off to the party at Radio Tokyo. The only topic of conversation was the Tokyo Bay monster – a stunt inspired by Orson Welles' 1938 radio broadcast of *The War of the Worlds*, which scared the living daylights out of Americans, who thought they were being invaded by aliens. But the monster joke backfired, with some of those responsible dismissed from headquarters and sent back to the States.

The longer she stayed in Japan, the more Mary became involved in the US Catholic Women's League, and she was eventually elected secretary. The league raised money for charities, including many of the Catholic schools and convents, hit hard by the war. The French Sacre Coeur nuns ran one of the two Catholic schools in Tokyo before the war, catering mainly to the diplomats and wealthy Japanese. During the occupation, Helen and Jim attended the Tokyo school. An Irish order ran the other school, which took in the poorer students. Both schools sustained damage from the Allied bombing, but the Irish nuns were the worst off – they slept on the floor and had no money for food. Mary and her friends looked for ways to raise money for the two convents.

Part III: Occupation

One of the first people I put on their list for charity (before Mary arrived) was Archbishop Paul Marella, whom I had found while roaming the streets of Tokyo for stories early in the occupation. In prewar Japan, as Rome representative, Marella had been given the privileges of a diplomat. Once Italy was defeated, he was refused permission to leave Japan and forced to fend for himself as food rations tightened. The house where he lived with another priest was bombed during a raid on Tokyo. The Japanese would not help the pair repair the house, so they lived among the ruins, cooking over a fire in the open and scrounging for food. When I met him, Archbishop Marella was sitting in a room at a table, dressed in a large overcoat and muffler, with his mittened hands clutching a large bottle of hot water. When the Catholic Women's League found him, they provided him with food, while I helped out with transportation. By the time Mary arrived, the league was more established, looking for more and more fundraising opportunities.

One of these was a film screening in a Japanese theatre to raise money for the nuns and the Japanese tuberculosis hospital. Mary had a contact, Charles Mayer, who represented Hollywood and the US film industry in the Far East. He agreed to give her a film called *The Song of Bernadette* (1943), as long as he didn't have to pay tax on it. Mary had her film, but getting the government to agree to remove the tax was another matter. Her first request was refused outright, even though the money went to Japanese Catholic nuns running a Japanese hospital. She went to the Diet to lobby members, roving from office to office, and at 5 pm that day, she found someone in the Japanese government who agreed to remove the tax.

The screening was held in one of Tokyo's largest theatres on Ginza. Japanese people queued to see the film and the house was full. The takings topped one million yen, and the government donated another two million yen.

Mary's money-raising skills were fast becoming known. One woman came to her with a new Chevrolet car, which had been sent to her by friends back home in the States. They were happy for the car to be used to raise money, so, after cutting through a bit of occupation red tape, Mary suggested a raffle. She got permission to sell the tickets outside the American department store, with the brand new Chevrolet parked on Ginza. Only Americans were allowed to buy tickets, and, in seven days, they raised their money with an American GI the proud new owner.

Gambling also proved a winner for the Catholic women. Their committee organised a gambling night, along with dancing and dinner, at the American officers' club. Colonel Mahoney was in charge of the club, which was situated in the best building in Tokyo. He agreed to Mary's proposition immediately and arranged food and liquor, which would be charged to the league. He found a young GI with an expert knowledge of gambling and an ambition to work in Las Vegas after the war. He taught a few volunteers, including myself, how to run a gaming table. I was no professional, but I raised a lot of money.

The night was a huge success, raising US$10 000 after all expenses were paid. The only sour note came from some officious army officers who complained that their club had been taken over by the US Catholic Women's League, and

Part III: Occupation

Colonel Mahoney was transferred to an army post as a reprimand. It didn't seem to worry him because he was retiring, but we felt guilty about the outcome.

Chapter Fourteen

Generals

Aboard the 'Octogonian' Express in 1946 when General Eisenhower visited Japan and toured with General Eichelberger. Photograph: US Eighth Army.

WHEN I MET HIM, I knew little about MacArthur's past. There has been much written about him, both negative and glowing. All I can add is that during my seven years under his command, I always found him impressive. He seemed the right man to command the war in the Pacific and oversee the occupation of Japan; he governed a vanquished country without any revenge or retaliation. The Japanese learned to love him.

From my first contact with the general, I realised he would be hard to get to know. He turned down picture requests on many occasions, particularly those that would involve his family. During the occupation, I had several interviews with him and faced the same routine. He met me at the door of the office, escorted me to a large easychair away from the desk – he never sat at his own desk when a visitor called – and he took the opposite chair. His desk did not even hold a telephone. His chief aide monitored all calls, and relayed messages to him. We got down to business immediately and he was prepared to give a little if asked reasonable questions. He was friendly and I felt at ease, but, each time, after thirty minutes, I would sense it was time to leave and the general would escort me to the door.

MacArthur was an enigma. The more I worked with him, the more I wanted to produce a full documentary on his life inside the embassy. I wanted to get behind his stoic personality and film him at home with his family. I had seen him striding up a beach in the Pacific under fire, but I had not filmed him playing with his son, Arthur. My reasons extended beyond the satisfaction of getting a good story that would have attracted wide release in the States. I wanted to record it as history because the man had played such a pivotal role in the century's biggest conflict.

During the occupation, he instituted a grinding schedule. General MacArthur and his family had taken over the original American Ambassador's residence, while he had his office in downtown Tokyo. Every morning, seven days a week, between 9 and 10 am, his driver would take him along a route lined with armed guards to his office. After working for two or three hours, he would lunch at the residence. Following his afternoon nap, the general returned to his office, where he worked until 8 or 9 pm.

Part III: Occupation

I told him my reasons for wanting to film him. I even pleaded, saying it would be for posterity. He refused. 'This is my home. It is very private. I want it that way. If I let you in Bill, I would be compelled to let every other camera crew inside the embassy.'

So I had to make do with recording his public face. Not long after we had established the Foreign Correspondents' Club, we invited MacArthur to the first official lunch. Much to our surprise, he accepted. The general rarely visited international residents, and some, such as General Derevyanko at the Soviet embassy, he never visited. He entertained very rarely, unlike General Eichelberger. We were honoured he accepted. He spoke mainly about the Allied victory over Japan.

Jean MacArthur, a poised and charming woman, was more forthcoming than her husband. But being a good diplomat, she would never have given anything away that could have embarrassed her husband. They appeared to adore each other.

Mary and I got to know Jean during the occupation. I first met her shortly after her husband spoke at the Foreign Correspondents' Club. The correspondents received an invitation to lunch at the embassy, with the only condition being no cameras. On arrival, we were checked twice by armed guards, once at the gates and once at the front door. Jean waited to greet us in a big hall and directed us to the reception room where we waited for the general, who was still at the office. At 1 pm, he walked straight into the room, kissed his wife, and then moved around to greet each correspondent personally. We were asked to move into the dining room, where a table was set for forty, plus the hosts.

Flickers of History

As the general moved to one end of the table, there was a rush for the seats on either side of him. I made it down the other end next to Jean, and I still think I got the best story. After a little small talk, Jean described in some detail their escape from Manila after the Japanese invasion.

As lunch finished, I realised the correspondent opposite me had hardly got a word in, for I had monopolised the hostess. I felt I got to know her that day. While talking, Jean kept her eye on her husband, and, at some secret signal, she rose, followed by the general, and led us out to say goodbye.

During the occupation, I followed MacArthur closely, as I had during the war. Wherever MacArthur went, there was a story. In 1946 I followed him to South Korea for an official visit to President Syngman Rhee – a visit that was news simply because the general rarely left Tokyo. When we arrived in Seoul, the general and his wife were given an official welcome. MacArthur sat on the dais, without a cap, for nearly two hours on one of the hottest days on record. That night the president and his wife hosted a lavish reception for the MacArthurs, to which we were all invited.

MacArthur was not the only remarkable person making news. There were many visits by officers and other high-profile characters. In May 1946, I read a small piece in the army newspaper about a planned visit by the Supreme Allied Commander of the European War, General Dwight David Eisenhower. It was bound to be interesting because before the war Eisenhower served on MacArthur's staff in Washington

Part III: Occupation

and the Philippines. They had not seen each other since Eisenhower left the Philippines before the war. By July 1943, Eisenhower had been promoted to full general. It was rumoured that Eisenhower wanted to fly to Japan to meet his old boss on equal terms. Being a combat veteran, MacArthur thought he had the upper hand over Eisenhower.

I knew such a visit would be handled by Eichelberger, who would take Eisenhower around Japan on his train, which he had dubbed The Eighth Army Octogonian Express. That was the pattern with all the VIPs who visited Japan. I asked Eichelberger to put me on the invitation list if the visit came off. He told me, 'If I get that job, you'll be the first to be invited.' True to his word, I got the call one night at the club. 'Do you still want to go on the trip with me when Eisenhower arrives?' Eichelberger asked. 'You're darn' tootin,' I replied.

Apart from a few of the old warcos from the Pacific, the correspondents took little notice of Eichelberger because he was in Yokohama, away from the main game. My regular contact with the general paid off. There was only room for six correspondents on the train with private sleeping quarters. Those who missed out complained bitterly until Eichelberger put on an extra carriage attached to a Japanese train service to take the other correspondents down to Kyoto to meet the official party. Those guys did not get the full trip, but they could not afford to be choosy.

The plane flew into Ebisu airport and when the door slid back and the steps were rolled in, out stepped the five-star-general, met by his old boss. My camera rolled from the moment Eisenhower stepped out the door, and I looked for any signs of tension as they met for the first time in years. They shook hands warmly. They seemed to be on good terms, but it was difficult to tell as they got into the car immediately, and I did not see Eisenhower until I boarded the train.

We stopped first at the Hotel Hakone, set in a beautiful mountainous area south of Tokyo – a cameraman's dream. The hotel was surrounded by forests and hot pools, which were staffed by women in elegant kimonos. The service was wonderful and everything, including massages, was on offer.

The Japanese manager had arranged a tea ceremony for General Eisenhower, a custom with which we had become familiar during our stay in Japan. It was held in a special room, with the floor covered in cushions for each of the guests to sit on. Japanese ladies, dressed in kimonos, set about making the tea from green powder and hot water. I took part in many tea ceremonies but never got used to the taste of the tea.

The tea was poured into small Japanese cups without handles, and one of the ladies took a cup over to General Eisenhower, bowing as she handed it to him. As he sipped the tea, another girl brought over a plate of sugar cakes, which were so sweet they would rot your teeth. The general thanked the women and didn't comment on the tea and cake, so I never knew whether he enjoyed it.

I had been shooting stills for my mate, Tom Shafer, who was stuck in Tokyo, as there was not enough light to shoot for the newsreel. When the ceremony was over, Eisenhower asked to see me outside. 'I would appreciate it if you didn't send any of those pictures back to the States,' he said. 'You know the feelings back there since the end of the war. If any of these

Part III: Occupation

pictures appeared in the press, the people wouldn't like seeing me fraternising with the enemy.' I responded, 'General, I'll show you what I'll do.' I took the negatives out of their holders and destroyed them. He could have ordered me to obey without so much as a smile, but given his polite request, I happily agreed.

That night there was a special dinner to honour the general and the army invited a guest entertainer, an Egyptian named Gilli Gilli, who swallowed live chickens, regurgitated them and placed them on a table in front of Eisenhower. He looked both surprised and disgusted, but the chickens looked fine. Apparently, during the First World War, the Australian troops in Egypt were entertained with the same act by a person with the same name.

Everyone slept on the train that night before travelling to the Nikko, another resort north of Tokyo. There was a dinner party at the hotel that night and, after dinner, we made our way back to the station. We found five GIs lined up at the station. The Japanese stationmaster stood there, holding a large watch and a whistle, waiting to blow it at precisely the right time. Throughout the trip, the stationmasters had been great sticklers for time. The whistle went and the train moved, no matter who was on or off.

Every time Eisenhower saw a GI, he asked him where he came from in the hope of finding someone from the same home town, Denison, Texas. He never found anyone in Japan. That night, he saw the soldiers and approached them to ask the usual question and, again, he had no luck. He carried on the conversation, asking whether they liked it in Japan, and whether they were getting good food.

Flickers of History

A young American with a high-pitched voice, said 'Yes sir, the food is good, but it's badly cooked'. The colonel in charge of the group nearly exploded, his face was so red. 'You had steak tonight, soldier,' he said firmly. 'No sir, we had pork chops,' the soldier replied. 'You had steak,' the colonel repeated, with his nostrils flaring by way of warning. 'No sir, we had pork chops,' he repeated. The more adamant he became, the higher his voice rose. Before the colonel could reply, Eisenhower butted in and said, 'Colonel, if the boy said he had pork chops, he would know he had pork chops.' He then spoke to the soldier. 'This is what I want you to do, son. I want you to write to me in Washington and give me all the facts about what you have told me. I will take action from the States.' He then turned back to the colonel, who by this time looked as if he would have a stroke. 'Furthermore Colonel,' Eisenhower added, 'I do not want anything to happen to this boy.'

The episode was dutifully reported back in the States and it became known as the Pork Chop Incident. For me, it showed Eisenhower could relate to GIs. The general was warm and sociable, and genuinely interested in people, whereas MacArthur was a much more private man. However, despite my original expectations of friction between MacArthur and Eisenhower, there seemed to be no animosity.

MacArthur's refusal to pose for pictures became legendary. We were always trying to think of ways to get him to relax for a decent amount of time for the camera. Sometimes visiting personalities helped. Father Edward Flanagan, who, in 1917 founded Boys Town, a community for underprivileged boys, visited Japan during the occupation. Father Flanagan became well known for his saying, 'there are no bad boys', and did an extraordinary job of transforming difficult boys into good citizens. Hollywood made a movie of his work, starring Spencer Tracy and Mickey Rooney.

I met Father Flanagan at Tokyo airport and explained MacArthur's intractability when it came to pictures. I knew MacArthur would meet Father Flanagan, escort him to his car after their interview and duck off before we had time to capture him on camera. The priest was happy to help and skilfully manoeuvred the general so we could secure some good shots. About halfway through the process, MacArthur realised what we were doing, grinned and stood still for the camera. At last, he had relented.

It all made for a good newsreel story and Father Flanagan wrote to thank me for the coverage, which made five newsreels worldwide. I heard later of his death in May 1948. While visiting Germany with his nephew, he suffered a heart attack. Sadly, language difficulties delayed medical help. After saying the last rites with the army chaplain, Father Flanagan died.

In June 1946, Lieutenant General Horace Robertson replaced another Australian lieutenant general, John Northcott, as the commander-in-chief of the British Commonwealth Occupation Force (BCOF). Known as Red Robbie, the new commander seemed to have an inferiority complex when it came to the Americans. The Australians did not have it as good as the

Americans, and their base in Kure was no match for Tokyo. BCOF had only one Japanese hotel, the Marunouchi, for their visitors. The Australians' food came from the British embassy, and a small army task force carried out their administration.

Red Robbie complained constantly about his lack of facilities. He wanted a special train like Eichelberger's to take him around Japan. He didn't seem to understand that it was primarily an American occupation and Eichelberger was second in charge. Even so, Eichelberger gave Robertson a special car that could be hooked up to the Japanese train system if he wanted to travel. Robertson then complained that the Australians did not have access to a holiday resort. Eichelberger gave him the magnificent Kawana Hotel on the Ito Peninsula in the hope it would shut him up. Guests of the first-class hotel had access to a superb golf course and sporting facilities.

Robertson showed his true colours when he went to visit MacArthur in Tokyo. After the meeting, he headed to the two elevators, one of which was manned by a Japanese boy, whose job was to hold the lift for MacArthur. Robertson got into the elevator and the Japanese boy said, 'Excuse me sir, this is General MacArthur's elevator. I am waiting for him.' Robbie flew into a rage and bent over to show the boy the three stars on his epaulet. 'Do you see these three crowns? They represent three stars, boy. Now take me down.'

The liftboy relented. One of MacArthur's staff saw the whole incident, and, as soon as the elevator disappeared, ran back to tell the general's chief aide. Robertson's popularity plummeted even further.

Part III: Occupation

The Allies were not the only high-ranking generals stationed in Japan. I met generals from other armies, including General Shang Chen, the chief of the Chinese mission in Japan. Mary and I went to many parties at the general's house, where we met many other Chinese generals. After establishing some good contacts, I travelled to Taiwan, then known as Formosa, to shoot a story on the Chinese Army in training. I arrived in Taipei and then caught a train which had a sleeping apartment to Kao-hsiung. I shared a two-bunk cabin with a young Chinese air force lieutenant, who wore a uniform that looked a lot like an American fly-boy's. It was a smooth trip.

A young Chinese lieutenant colonel, Shen Ching, who was aide to General Sun Le Ren, the deputy commander-in-chief of the Chinese Army at Formosa, met me at the station. In a heavy American accent, Shen told me that 7 am was a little early to meet the general and offered me some breakfast in the station restaurant. It reminded me of the stations in country NSW I visited when I was a boy, so the offer of bacon, eggs, buttered toast and coffee was the best invitation I had heard for a long time. He apologised because they only had duck eggs, which had a stronger taste than chicken eggs, but that didn't bother me. I was hungry enough to eat anything – or so I thought.

We sat at a table near the door to the kitchen and listened to the sounds of sizzling eggs and the smell of bacon and coffee – a wonderfully sentimental smell. When the meal arrived, it was not as I had imagined, and my stomach backflipped when I saw it. The large eggs swam in a puddle of fat, as did the bacon. The toast was smeared with an axle grease similar to what the Australian army used to try to pass off as butter during the war. There was nothing else to do but eat what was before me. I waded into it, drinking copious amounts of coffee to wash it down. At least the coffee was hot, although the taste was another thing.

When we arrived at the camp, General Sun was waiting for us. He was a tall, good-looking man, impeccably dressed in a uniform that fitted him perfectly and displayed many war decorations.

After I explained what I wanted to shoot, he changed into his fatigues and drove to the training area. Barbed wire hung between wooden posts to make a dangerous net, which lay only a foot above the ground. The men were ordered to get down on their bellies and crawl, while carrying their rifles, under the barbed wire. At the other end of the wire, two machine-guns fired live bullets over the heads of the men. It all looked a bit too dangerous, even if the men were wearing steel helmets. I could only assume the soldiers had done this before and were familiar with the exercise.

General Sun took me to the officers' mess for lunch, where flies circled plates of tired cabbage, spinach and chopped meat. He steered me over to a table and took a chair next to me. Struggling with chopsticks, I eventually finished my meal, but General Sun loaded up my plate with more food, using his own chopsticks. I expected to drink Chinese tea, but we were served hot water, which I found refreshing because it helped wash the food down and settle my queasy stomach.

A siesta after lunch formed part of the daily ritual. General Sun led me to another building for the officers, furnished with benches each with their own Chinese headrest. The rest was

Part III: Occupation

curved, allowing the neck to rest in the bend. I never thought I would get off to sleep because they looked so uncomfortable but I dropped off without any trouble.

In two hours, we were up again and I shot more pictures of troops training in the field. I returned to the general's house after the shoot to shower and change for dinner. We had a drink in his bar before being served an eight-course supper, which included a beautiful dish of duck in ginger sauce. I awaited dessert with a mix of anticipation and apprehension.

Huge platters of watermelon arrived, which were very tempting in such a hot climate. With no plates provided, I didn't know what to do with the seeds, so I took my cue from the general. He picked up a large slice and began eating it as if he were playing the harmonica, only he made a sucking noise. He spat the seeds straight onto the white table cloth, and I had no choice but to follow his lead.

I met many generals during the war and the occupation, but MacArthur remained the role model for the ordinary soldier. In the First World War it was said he was fearless in times of danger. He was known to crawl out of his foxhole at night, without a helmet, to attack the machine-gun nests behind enemy lines. He was decorated for such acts of bravery and, in those early days, the acclaim made him cocky and vain. MacArthur seemed to have matured and mellowed by the Second World War, though he remained fearless at the front line. I saw him stand his ground under enemy fire without flinching. He rode through the war triumphantly to take on the

Flickers of History

formidable task of administering the occupation and became the so-called 'uncrowned emperor' of Japan.

MacArthur's fifty-two years of military service came to an abrupt end on 11 April 1951, when Truman dismissed him – from his command of all UN forces in Korea and from the direction of the occupation forces in Japan – for publicly criticising US policy on the Korean War. He learned of the decision from an aide who had been listening to a radio bulletin.

When the seventy-one-year-old general returned to the United States for the first time since 1937, millions turned out to welcome him home. MacArthur accepted an invitation from Congress to address a joint session. On 19 April 1951, he made an eloquent and dramatic speech, which ended with the memorable line, 'old soldiers never die, they just fade away'. He died in 1964, aged eighty-four, in Washington DC, and is buried in Norfolk, Virginia. There will never be another Douglas MacArthur.

Chapter Fifteen

The Japanese

Bill Carty with the King of Japan. Bill holds up a priceless string of pearls belonging to the king. Photograph: Tom Shaper, United Press.

ONCE MY FAMILY ARRIVED, life in Japan seemed more permanent, and it certainly felt more complete. In the past, Japan had always felt like a temporary posting, as though I should never get too comfortable because I would soon rejoin my family in Australia. With them in Japan, I could concentrate on work but also enjoy a home life that I had missed for five years.

Although family life gave me a new focus, I maintained my quota of at least three newsreel stories a week. I worked

Flickers of History

directly with the news director, Ted Genock, who passed on appreciative messages from the other bosses. I remember once being told that I was the most productive pool cameraman in the world at the time.

At the beginning of the occupation, the stories revolved around the Allied powers and their role in Japan. These newsreels are a few examples.

The EYES and EARS of the WORLD
– Paramount News presents

RENOUNCE WAR - MACARTHUR
Tokyo – Appearing before the Allied Control Commission, Gen. Douglas MacArthur commends the Jap renunciation of war and urges all nations to follow suit. He reviews his occupation policy and reaffirms his plans for democracy in Japan.

WORLD's BIGGEST G.I. STORE!
Tokyo – The largest store for GIs in the world, the new Army Post Exchange, opens its doors to the men of our occupation forces, with five million dollars worth of stock on hand.

NIPPON VOTES!
Japan's first free general elections, most important event in the democratic reconstruction of the defeated country. Japanese women storm polls as they receive the right to vote. Widespread political demonstrations are signs of a new political awakening in Japan.

Part III: Occupation

The Allied occupation and the accompanying fallout from the war weren't the only stories in Japan. So much was new to the rest of the world. Outside the major cities and towns lived people largely untouched by the new forces running the country. Japanese culture was totally foreign to many — the Japanese way of life provided a source of great interest to the outside world.

The Japanese also showed interest in me. They were aware of Paramount, which had screened newsreels in Japan before the war. Many knew the slogan, 'the eyes and ears of the world', and the logo of the cameraman winding the camera to film. In the city, people would rush up to me in the street when I was filming, and wind the camera as they had seen at the start of the newsreels.

Many of the non-war stories documented the natural disasters that struck Japan. The country seemed prone to any form of catastrophe that nature, or sometimes man, produced. Just after I arrived with the occupation forces, a fire swept through a number of blocks in Yokohama. I got down there to witness firefighters trying to put out a raging fire with a hose that dribbled a miserable trickle of water. The Allied bombing had wrecked the city's plumbing, and the Americans were not rushing to help. In the end, the firefighters could do little but watch until the flames died down.

Later in the first year, I heard of an island that had mysteriously appeared two hundred miles south of Tokyo. It was only fifty miles from the mainland, so I organised for a plane to take me down to film it. Sure enough, a small island had come out of the sea, caused by something below. The water swirled around it, hot and disturbed, as if the sea itself knew the island was not meant to be there. I shot my film and left. Within three days the island had disappeared.

Then came another natural phenomenon. An old volcano blew its top on Sakurajima on Kyushu in March 1946. Rocks the size of jeeps were thrown out of the mountain, and fiery lava flowed around its base towards the villages. As the people were evacuated, I leaned on my contacts in the Fifth Air Force and organised a plane to take Tom Shafer and me down to Kyushu, Japan's southernmost island. A colonel, who was a real shutterbug, decided to fly us down himself.

The view from the plane made a spectacular picture. As soon I saw the huge glowing rocks being tossed into the air, I knew the film would get a good run on the newsreels. We landed at the nearest army camp and organised a jeep to take us as far in as possible. The intense heat prevented us from getting too close. The best pictures were available from the air, so we took a final pass over the volcano before heading home.

The first major disaster during my Japan stint was the earthquake which hit the city of Fukui in June 1948. I had a taste of earth tremors not long after I had arrived in Tokyo. The Foreign Correspondents' Club had just been finished when the windows and doors began shaking. With nowhere to go, I felt helpless. I remembered the pictures I had seen of the Tokyo earthquake in 1923 and the reports of the death toll.

So I had a small idea of what the people of Fukui must have felt. At 6 pm Mary and I greeted our three dinner guests on the night of the quake. They were Australian priests who had volunteered for a five-year term of missionary work. Roast lamb with mint sauce – a typical Australian dinner – was to be their first meal in Japan. Just as we had sat down, the table started shaking. Although frightened, I knew the quake was not in the Tokyo area. I forgot the lamb and spent the next hour trying to track down exactly where it was.

As Fukui was a long way south of Tokyo, I again called on the Fifth Air Force to find a plane to fly up to thirty correspondents down to the disaster area. We were to meet at Ebisu airport, so I contacted the club to spread the word that a plane would leave at midnight.

It took three hours to reach the devastated city. After a late start, we flew over Fukui at 5 am, and the plane's first pass gave us time to evaluate the damage. From the air, it looked as though the city had been extensively bombed. Fires had swept through the place and the smell of burning flesh flew in through the open door as we began filming. Satisfied with our aerial shots, we headed to a landing strip twenty-five miles out of the city – the only one large enough to take a transport plane. At the nearby army camp, we took in the details of the disaster over breakfast. With all vehicles banned from the area, we began the long hike into the heart of the city.

The scene reminded me of the war. The official death toll stood at close to four thousand, but after picking through the scene, I was sure it was a conservative estimate. For a start, two buildings, the Catholic church on the edge of the city and the movie theatre, were completely full at the time of the quake and both buildings were completely demolished. No one in either building survived.

I shot extensive film of the aftermath, but my pictures were not the best. *Life* and *Time* photographer Carl Mydans, whom

Flickers of History

I knew from the war, happened to be staying at a military unit on a special assignment when the earthquake hit Fukui. His pictures were given a four-page spread and made the cover of *Life* magazine.

Carl later told me he was eating dinner with a group when the quake struck – the plates slid off, and the food fell to the floor. He ran outside to see what was happening, then rushed back in to grab his gear. Carl began shooting as he ran towards the city. Telegraph poles bent like matchsticks before breaking, and buildings crashed to the ground. Despite his extensive coverage, he wished for a movie camera. He told me, 'Bill, if you had been there at the time, you would have had the scoop of your life. You could have got the best action pictures ever.'

That is how it is for the cameraman. You have to be there at the time, otherwise there is no story. 'If only I had been there' is a common refrain, but you realise by the end of your career that you had your fair share of breaks. Fukui was Carl's big break – actually it was one of a number of Carl's breaks. He was one of *Life's* best photographers during the war. He and his wife Shelley, who was also a photographer, had been prisoners in Santo Tomas in the Philippines, and were only released after Washington agreed to an exchange of prisoners.

The other impressive footage of Fukui belonged to Japanese photographer, James Haratani, who was also in the city at the time. He took colour slides that captured the crumbling structures, including the collapse of a bridge and a department store. He also captured more poignant shots, such as a little girl clutching a doll in the ruins of her home. His pictures of the human reaction to the disaster were depressingly dramatic.

Tokyo's first floods hit early one Sunday morning in 1948. My family and I were leaving mass when I got word that the emperor was going by boat to inspect the floods. The kids had not eaten breakfast, but I decided against driving them back home because it would take too much time. With my gear already in the car, I bundled the kids in and drove off to find the emperor.

The occupation forces were unaffected by the flooding, which had struck low-lying areas filled with shacks that had been built by the poor following the surrender. I found the royal party and went to board the boat, but Hirohito's security guards would not let me anywhere near him. I was directed to a second boat, tied up behind his. The captain took off after the emperor as my hungry children began a chorus of complaints. There was nothing to eat on board the boat, not even a glass of water for freeloaders like us, so the kids would just have to wait.

Their attention shifted to the Japanese families, who stood on the roofs of their houses, with their animals – chickens, dogs and pigs – surrounded by water, lapping at the eaves. Some had dragged a few belongings up to the roof, but they had nothing to eat and their rescuers had not yet arrived with supplies. They made a pathetic picture for my camera. We saw family after family, but there wasn't a supply boat in sight.

As the emperor sailed past, the people struggled to their feet to bow and he bowed in return, but there was not a word of sympathy, as he passed by in silence, before returning to the dock.

Meanwhile, my children's temporary silence ended. They started up again in earnest, whining of thirst and hunger and when I got them home, they raided the icebox. I was sent to Coventry for putting the family to such inconvenience, but it didn't bother me. I was accustomed to going without food for stories, and New York was pleased with the pictures.

South-west of Tokyo there is a seaport town called Wakayama. As its residents slept one night, a huge tidal wave swept over the houses, filling the passages and streets with water before reversing at incredible speed, sucking people back into the sea. It then lurched forward again, swallowing the town, before spitting it out once more and claiming more lives.

The full death count was unknown. The tidal wave at Wakayama was another one of those inexplicable natural events in Japan that made me think of Australia. As I picked over the sodden city with Carl Mydans, I tried to imagine how Sydneysiders would cope if such a wave hit Bondi, a similarly densely populated area by the sea. The Japanese kept picking themselves up after disasters and rebuilding.

It was not all death and mayhem. I produced many stories on the Japanese way of life, particularly in the latter years of the occupation, as the shadow of the war faded. Often I would take my family to introduce them to some element of the Japanese culture which I had witnessed. I thought it was important, especially for my children's education. Not long after my family arrived, I visited the Miki Moto pearl farm.

Miki was eighty-seven when I met him in 1946. His quiet and likeable manager and publicity officer, Kata San, took me down to the pearl farm on the first visit. Kata San had everything planned down to the last detail for the long train ride down to the Bay of Ago. I knew the train stopped at some of the bigger towns for ten minutes, but was shocked when ushered out of the train to meet a party of Japanese –

the stationmaster, the chief of police, the mayor and even the chief butcher of the town. We moved down the row, shaking hands and bowing, before being taken inside the station house for tea and cakes. When the train was ready to leave, we shook hands, bowed again, and were escorted back to our car. The same thing happened in two more towns before we reached our destination.

From the moment I met Miki, I thought him remarkable. He was born in 1858, the eldest of nine children, which was an unusually large family for the Japanese. He produced his first cultured pearl in 1893, after he and his wife Ume had conducted extensive experiments. Ume died after fifteen years of marriage, leaving Miki with five children and the germ of a business. They had just begun putting cultured pearls onto the world market. Broken-hearted over her death, he struggled on, eventually becoming a multimillionaire. Devoted to the memory of his wife, he never remarried.

When I arrived at the farm, I was shown to the guesthouse on one of his two islands. It consisted of comfortable spotless Japanese-style quarters with a futon mattress, which was set-up every night under a mosquito net. There was a big round wooden tub filled with hot water for my bath, and a traditional Japanese toilet with no seat.

His farm holdings, which totalled more than forty thousand acres, took in the two islands and the waters of the Bay of Ago. Miki lived on an island where he cultivated his pearls, which, before the war, had brought in US$50 million from the United States alone. The war had all but destroyed his business with the huge American market, but he was determined to build it

Flickers of History

up to the same levels before he died. With this goal in mind, he flew two flags on his island – the Japanese and the American. Miki, who had a natural flair for publicity, was a real showman.

I was taken across to Miki's island from the guesthouse island, where I received a warm welcome. Even though he was small and wiry, I could tell he was fit by just looking at him. I discovered he swam between the two islands and back every day as part of his exercise regime. He showed me a fine pearl necklace, worth US$250 000 and earmarked for Crown Prince Akihito, which was the result of twenty years' work. It featured a huge pearl, the size of a plum, in the centre of the strand, surrounded by graduated pearls.

After telling me his life story, Miki took me to see the diving girls in action. These young, solidly built Japanese women were excellent swimmers, who could stay under water for long periods with only a normal glass diving snorkel. They were employed to collect the oysters, which were not attached to rocks but simply lay on the sea bed. They scoured the bottom of the bay with a net bag, filling it with oysters. When they had a full load, they resurfaced and emptied the bag into a wooden pail, which was attached by a length of rope tied around the diver's waist. The pail floated on the surface of the water, carrying the day's catch. The divers became a highlight of the pearl farm, attracting tourists from around the world.

On the island, a second team of women were trained to implant the seed pearl in the oysters to create the cultured pearl. Miki had developed a technique of opening the oyster without breaking the neck. It was fascinating to watch the whole process, although he would never explain to me exactly how it was done. Sitting at individual desks, the women placed an oyster on a small stand, prised it open, and placed a small wooden peg between the shell to keep it open. Taking a scalpel from a set that looked like a dentist's kit, the women would make a small incision in what Miki said was the oyster's kidney. After the seed pearl was placed in the incision, a small sliver from another oyster was placed over the seed. Once the peg was removed, the oyster was thrown into a tray, to allow it to close. The holding trays were then dropped into the water. The oysters were brought to the surface every three months to clean away any moss or weed on the shells.

Natural oysters are usually formed from grit that causes irritation and creates the pearl. Miki's cultured pearls took between three and five years to grow, allowing him to control the creation of pearls.

As lunchtime approached, Miki invited me into a large room to sit down. His staff, all of whom were there, placed a small table in the middle of the room. I was wondering what was going on, when Miki sat in the middle of the table. The women started cheering, and then the wiry old man neatly curled his feet around his neck, and lifted himself up on his hands. The act required incredible strength. As he held himself in midair, the women clapped even more enthusiastically, as did I, and Miki soaked up the attention. He loved every minute of it.

A platter of oysters arrived for lunch. My host sat opposite me and began eating, so I followed his lead and took a bite of an oyster. My teeth hit something hard, so I spat it out to see whether I had hit the shell but it was a cultured pearl. Miki began laughing and when he saw the shock on my face, he became hysterical. The next five oysters all had a pearl inside. I was working my way up to a necklace. Then came the fried oysters, which looked very tempting. I thought I would be clear with cooked oysters, thinking they would not contain a pearl, but one bite and I was spitting pearls back onto the plate. By the end of the meal, which also included lobsters, I had twelve beautiful cultured pearls.

I stayed with Miki for three days during that first visit. As a natural entertainer, he loved being followed by a camera. The story made it to all five American newsreels and the publicity gave Miki the boost that he needed to increase his business. When I told General Eichelberger about the amazing Miki Moto, he asked me to take him and his wife down to the farm, with my wife Mary. We also took MacArthur's wife, Jean, Eichelberger's second in charge, Major General Clovis Byers, and his wife and aides. We travelled in style on the general's train. With his usual enthusiasm, Miki greeted us like old friends, lavishing the party with gifts of pearl rings, necklaces, bracelets and earrings. Miki made a great fuss over Mary because of the story I had shot. As a result of our visit, the American PX store filled its shelves with pearl products, much to Miki's delight.

Another Japanese industry that interested me was the beautiful enamelware known as cloisonné. The Americans were crazy about the stuff, and, before the war, much of it was shipped to the United States. One of the biggest factories was in Nagoya, a few hours from Tokyo by air. With Eichelberger's permission, Mary and I travelled to Nagoya, where we were met by our liaison officer. We were billeted with the army, which provided all of our meals, plus a car and a driver.

The general manager made a great fuss when we arrived and showed us into his office for tea, which was a ritual for all Japanese businesses. Near the office stood a dining table, beautifully set with the porcelain from the factory. Displayed on the plates was a full western meal of steak, fried eggs and vegetables.

I set up the lights and equipment and began filming the production process. The workers squatted on the floor, setting up different patterns on vases using thin strips of metal. The pieces emerged from the oven as highly polished vases and dishes.

Once I finished the filming, we were escorted to the dining table for lunch, which had been served four hours earlier. Both of us had assumed the meal we saw on the way in was a display, designed to sell the dinner service. Not wanting our hosts to lose face, I told the general manager that we only ever ate a full meal at night, never in the middle of the day. He didn't seem to mind when I said a sandwich with coffee or a beer would be fine for us.

The second factory, Choaichi, made Narumi china, and was in the next prefecture. There I filmed the whole process by which stone was ground into a powder before being turned into porcelain. Whole dinner sets were made up, baked in the kiln, then handpainted and baked again. The story, 'From dust to a dinner set', got a good run back in America. A week after we returned home, a large wooden box arrived at our door. It contained a twelve-piece Narumi dinner set. The whole set, minus one cup, has survived and has been handed down to our daughter Patricia.

Flickers of History

Later, I took my son Jim down to Gifu, a popular holiday resort town in central Honshu. Between May and October, people came to watch the traditional art of cormorant fishing on the Nagaragawa River, which runs down from the Dainichiga-take mountain. The cormorants wore tight collars around the lower part of their necks, which prevented them from eating the small river fish they were trained to catch. This method, which has been used for centuries, attracted large numbers of tourists, who watched from small boats decorated with beautiful coloured lights.

In the morning, the birds were carried in wicker baskets to the water, where they were loaded onto boats for their ride up the river. Men hauled the boats by rope along a track by the river, straining to pull them against the fast flowing current to the fishermen's starting point. The trek took most of the day. The heavy timber boats were each fitted with a pole on the bow, from which a small metal basket hung. A fire in the basket lured the fish.

At dusk, the boats set off downstream, each controlled by two fishermen. One man steered while the other controlled twelve birds, tied to his fingers by strong cord. He tossed them into the water, lit up by the flames and sparks shooting from the wire basket. The birds dived down into the water, and, when they surfaced with a fish in their mouth, fishermen pulled them on board to disgorge the fish, before tossing the birds overboard again.

The activity made a weird and wonderful spectacle, and I was thrilled to see my son enjoying it so much. As I filmed, the sightseeing boats assembled at the mouth of the river in Ise Bay.

Part III: Occupation

The fishing boats first appeared as sparks, like those shooting from the wire baskets, but, as they moved downstream, the tourists could slowly make out the details of the birds and their masters. When the boats finally entered the bay and glided to a stop, the visitors – talkative from the saki – cheered the fishermen as they put their birds back into the wicker baskets under the dying light of the fire.

Chapter Sixteen

Far East

Cameramen and journalists in the saloon of the US Lakeland Victory *getting their stories ready to send back to the USA from the coast of China.*

OCCUPIED JAPAN was not the only big story in what we used to call the Far East. While we were all consumed with the rebuilding of Japan, there were many other stories in the region. In May 1948, I travelled to Korea for the first free elections.

Working out of the Chosen Hotel in Seoul, each day I followed the candidates and filmed the authorities as they prepared for polling day. On the morning of the election, I filmed a group of nuns entering the polling booths at 7 am before mayhem broke out. By the end of the day, my footage formed an interesting collage of diverse images: I filmed riot squads beating up suspected communist terrorists, while women lined up to vote with babies strapped to their backs. I was thrilled with the coverage and received a letter from my bosses at Paramount:

> A merited word of congratulations for an outstanding news job . . . we have rarely seen a case where the newsreel camera did a better job than it did at the Korean elections . . . the result was one of the better newsreel clips of the year . . . as for your camera work, Bill, let us say you left very little to be desired.

Meanwhile, China was engaged in a civil war that would bring the communists to power in 1949. I could not cover the daily action of Mao Zedong and his Red Army, but I travelled around China to shoot a number of newsreels for world audiences. The vastness of the country fascinated me, and I was always on the lookout for potential stories.

Shanghai, the most comsopolitan of the Chinese cities, was the most popular port for foreigners. I flew in there in 1948. In response to the communist advances, Chiang Kai-shek's army took every available boat to Taiwan. I travelled in a US Army plane that flew so low on approach to Shanghai airport that it looked as though the pilot planned to land on the red-tiled roofs. I kept thinking of the mess it would make if we crashed.

The communists sat just thirty miles from Shanghai, apparently biding their time. I was warned to be careful about filming the armies on either side. Filming Chiang Kai-shek's army would have been particularly dangerous, as they would not have taken kindly to foreign cameramen taking pictures of their retreat. I got around it by setting up my camera on a tall building to shoot the action below.

The Foreign Correspondents' Club was at the top of the Bund Hotel, overlooking Soo-Chow Creek. Every morning I could watch the life below on the creek, which was full of barges, tied to one another, creating a large living platform. Many families never seemed to leave their floating homes. In the morning, they began their day with their ablutions at one end and their cooking at the other, while children and animals wandered the decks.

The Chinese police kept a sharp eye on these boat people. Many times I saw families marched onto the deck by the police, who would order them to kneel while they searched the barge, usually looking for drugs or stolen goods. If anyone moved during the search, they would be kicked by the cop.

The Bund which ran down by the river was the main drag. From early morning until late at night people walked along the street. A lot of trucks used the road too. Many of the vehicles had guards travelling with the driver to keep the thieves off the load. Particularly vulnerable were trucks carrying bales of cotton, and the guards carried large sticks to beat off the thieves. Marauders would jump aboard a truck, rip a hole in a bale and pull out great handfuls of cotton or wool, presumably to line their jackets for the freezing winter. The most effective thieves hunted in teams. Three men would run alongside a truck, each one occupying the guard, while the others snatched the goods.

One of my colleagues in Shanghai was a Chinese MGM cameraman known as Newsreel Wong, a personal friend of Chiang Kai-shek's. He invited me for dinner at his home, where his wife cooked a beautiful Chinese meal. Wong told me of the Chinese resentment towards the British, who treated them like second-class citizens, refusing to allow them in certain areas, such as public parks and banks. He knew the communists would have the support to take over, and MGM had told him to get out of Shanghai before they moved in, but Wong insisted on staying. 'Where would I go? This is my home and my work is here,' he told me that night. I never found out what happened to him but his life would have been worthless had the communists found out about his friendship with Chiang Kai-shek.

Before the communists came to power, a group of French nuns had formed a mission in the walled city in Shanghai. They became known for their work with the so-called basket babies – baby girls who had been dumped because they were born with some blemish or disability, making them a liability for a poor family. Some were thrown into the river, others were left to die on garbage heaps. The nuns employed a Chinese man to collect the baby girls and transport them back to the mission in a basket on the back of his bicycle. Every day he would cycle around the city's garbage dumps, on the lookout for babies who had survived the night. The dead ones were left where he found them. The survivors were reared in the mission and then taught to sew. The mission paid for their care by selling the beautiful embroidery created by the girls. They made ecclesiastical vestments and altar linen, as well as luncheon sets, delicate lingerie, panels, kimonos and other handiwork.

Part III: Occupation

Newsreel Wong alerted the world to the basket babies. My coverage focused on the babies once they had grown into women. Once they reached a certain age, the girls were allowed to leave, but many stayed on because they were provided with a home and three meals a day. The mission was closed when the communists took Shanghai, and I never found out what happened to the nuns or the girls.

Later, I headed to a city called Tsingtso (now known as Qingdao), north of Shanghai on the eastern coast of China, to shoot a story on the peanut industry, which had provided America with most of its peanuts before the war. I had read about the old Chinese custom of foot binding, where the foot is bound so that it is little more than a stump. After the war, the custom died out, but I thought I might be able to find some old women who had been subjected to this treatment as girls.

Having no luck in the city, I hired a car and driver to travel into the countryside. The landscape was like a desert, as the trees had all been cut down for firewood. Miles outside Tsingtso I found a walled village with an entrance on one side and an exit on the other. The car had to slow to a crawl to avoid the pigs, chickens, dogs and ducks that rambled about the village. The smell from these animals and the open drains was disgusting. The little outpost provided good footage of village life in China. Outside the walls, I saw a blind man, walking with the aid of a long pole. He looked like a character from biblical times, striding out with purpose.

We kept driving until the landscape changed. The countryside was covered in bushes, and, in the distance, I noticed an old woman walking with a peculiar gait, as she carried a bundle of firewood across her shoulders. It looked as though she had no feet. As I jumped out of the car and pointed my camera at her, she screamed abuse and, when I concentrated on her feet, her protests grew even louder. She hobbled quite quickly on her stumps and disappeared down the road we had just travelled. It wasn't much footage but at least I had some evidence of the old custom. I could not imagine how parents could put their little girls through such pain for a custom. I felt sorry for those kids and wanted to show how it affected their lives – right into their old age.

On my last trip before the takeover, I flew into Shanghai airport with F. H. Bartholomew, the vice-president of United Press. The airport was full of Chinese waiting to be evacuated, their baggage strewn around the airport lounge. Dozens of planes sat on the airstrip as immigration officers struggled to collect taxes in money not worth the paper it was printed on. Confusion reigned.

As I approached customs, I knew it was going to be a bad day. Customs officers immediately confiscated all of my raw stock – two thousand feet of negative. I was not allowed in the country until I paid $2.1 million Shanghai dollars, which is not as expensive as it sounds. My American dollars were unacceptable. Given that you needed a suitcase to carry US$100 worth of Chinese currency, it was not practical money with which to travel.

So began a surreal scene with customs officers, where they would argue for a while, walk away to have a cigarette and a chat with their fellow officers, before returning to begin the argument all over again. I was there for two hours before an SOS call to Northwest Airlines got me off the hook.

The management stepped in to settle the account, paying the officers great wads of dollars wrapped in rubber bands.

On the same flight, two Russian couriers, Grigori Prokine and Ivan Titov, carried packages under official seal. So concerned about their massive packages – and so distrustful of the baggage handling service – they booked extra seats for them. When they arrived at customs, they slipped right through, disappearing into the crowd. Intrigued to know what they were doing, I made enquiries, but only found their names.

We faced more trouble on the bus for the four-mile journey to the city. We were stopped for four hours at a barbed-wire roadblock manned by armed Nationalist soldiers. Every person was checked over before we were allowed to proceed. Bartholomew sent back a story on the whole ordeal for a New York paper, so my bosses found out about my exploits in their city newspaper.

As the communists prepared to march into Shanghai, foreigners had to decide whether to stay. Friends with Northwest Airlines urged me to stay to get some pictures, but I was unwilling to take the risk. If something happened to me, there was no one to look after my family, and I had already put Mary through too much trauma during the Pacific War to ask her to cope by herself while I entered a civil war zone.

Six months after the communists took over, we heard the stories about those who stayed on. The Americans were ordered to leave, so a ship was sent to Shanghai to pick up those who remained. They stopped at Tokyo, where they were treated to the first of many welcome home parties at which they described the first months of communist China.

Flickers of History

When the communists took over Shanghai, the Northwest employees were not allowed to close their office, even though no planes were allowed to land. They were ordered to keep on the Chinese staff and pay them in American dollars every week. The American staff had to turn up every day, even though there was nothing to do, and, on the weekends, they were confined to their apartment block, which at least had a pool and tennis court. So for six months, they did nothing but swim and play tennis.

Any Chinese considered rich were treated badly. Those Chinese living in the same block of apartments as the Americans weren't surprised when four soldiers burst into their home as part of the inspections made of all buildings in Shanghai. Some of the men were playing the Chinese game of mah jong, considered by the communists to be a game of the rich. One of the men got up to offer the soldiers some tea, but was promptly told to sit down. 'You like to play mah jong, so play mah jong,' one soldier ordered the men. The soldiers kept these four men sitting at the table, playing mah jong for two days without food, only allowing them to leave to go to the toilet or to get a glass of water.

The American Ambassador, Angus Ward, had no such luck. He was abducted by the communists, held in jail in Mukden (now Shenyang) for twelve months, and in solitary confinement for the final month, surviving on bread and water. While the communists talked of execution, Ward's staff and his wife were confined to the ambassador's residence.

Washington began negotiations for his release and finally applied enough pressure to force the communists to let him

Part III: Occupation

go in December 1949 – it was never going to be easy. The Americans sent a ship, the *Lakeland Victory*, with me and eleven other correspondents on board, to pick him up from a Chinese port. Meanwhile, Ward, his wife, their staff and several cats were bundled onto a train carriage at Mukden. During the seven-day train journey, they were not allowed to open the windows or the blinds, and there was only a basin in which to wash.

Having lost sixty pounds during his ordeal, Ward was gaunt and drawn. The prisoners were escorted to our ship by armed soldiers, but before the ambassador was allowed to board, he was asked to sign a document stating his family had arrived safely on the ship. Ward did not trust the communists. If he signed before he went aboard, he could be taken back to China once the communists had evidence proving they had carried out their part of the deal. A two-hour argument ensued.

While that was going on, I had convinced a young Chinese guard to pose for some pictures. No more than fourteen and proud of himself, he looked like any other grinning kid, except that he was strung with ammunition belts. I gave him a packet of cigarettes for his troubles and he went off happily.

Unloading my film in my cabin, there was a knock at the door from our captain. He said the Chinese colonel had been told I had photographed one of his men, and demanded my film. The boat could not leave the dock until I handed it over. Ward had come to an agreement, so I was the only hold-up. I handed over three rolls of unexposed negative, which seemed to satisfy both of them. We sailed past cliffs on which, we were told, soldiers waited ready to fire. The captain warned us that we

Flickers of History

would not be out of danger for another three hours, which left me wondering how long it would take them to develop the film.

The boat arrived safely in Pusan, Korea, where some of the television cameramen had chartered a plane to fly their film back to Tokyo, leaving me in danger of being scooped. There were no planes available at the nearest airport, so I found the Korean army base. With much sign language, a Korean pilot agreed to take me on his flight to Seoul in a single-engine plane. In three hours, we flew over some of the most depressing country I had ever seen.

From Seoul, my film was sent to New York on a flight that had come from Tokyo – the same plane that was carrying the television film belonging to my colleagues.

Chapter Seventeen

Farewell

Jim and Bill Carty with Arthur and Jean MacArthur at the American embassy in Tokyo, 1948.

THE REALITY OF WAR, which was a mixture of experiences at times surreal, mundane, heroic, painful and fateful, heightened my appreciation of the gift of life. After the war, the occupation seemed unreal and the happy times were intensified by the knowledge that these new experiences could not last forever. The friendships I made during those days lasted long after our last meetings, and I kept in touch with many of those I met until they died. My time in Japan changed dramatically when my family joined me. The occupation forces became more like a normal community once spouses and children were added to the equation, although we never lost sight of the unusual circumstances in which we lived – we knew it was never going to last forever. With Japan getting back on its feet, there was a feeling in the occupation forces that the job was done. We began thinking about going home.

General Eichelberger was the first of our close friends to leave. In 1948, he retired to Asheville, North Carolina. He began by farewelling the Eighth Army, which was under his command for four years beginning in September 1944. A more private farewell, which I attended, was held for his friends at his home at Yokohama. We reflected on the times in the New Guinea jungle, where I had first met Bob, then a two-star general.

On the day he left, the Japanese lined the road leading to the dock, where a ship would take Eichelberger back to the United States. The US provost marshal for Tokyo lent me his beautiful Buick roadster with a driver to follow the general's car down to the ship. All the way down, Eichelberger's car stopped to say goodbye to those Japanese he knew personally. When it came time for me to say farewell, my eyes filled with tears because I knew I would not see him again.

The arrival of television accelerated my decision to leave Japan. The box had hit America by the mid 1940s, and the days of the newsreels were numbered. The era of watching news on the silver screen ended as cinema companies began making the transformation from 35 mm film to 16 mm film. For people like me, who had worked on the silent pictures and then sound, it marked a sad time. I was not afraid of the new medium, for I had made technological leaps before. I just believed many people loved seeing the news on the big screen. Somehow it seemed more real.

When it closed down its newsreel, Paramount asked me to stay on as a freelance cameraman, but I declined. I could not afford to keep my family in Tokyo on the uncertainty of freelance cheques. Besides, it was a natural break for me and time for my family to return to our own country. Like many others, I made arrangements to leave.

When I went to say goodbye to General MacArthur, we chatted about the Australian troops, Australia and my association with the occupation. Right on thirty minutes, it was time for me to go, and he escorted me to the door and shook my hand. Later, Mary and I were invited to afternoon tea at the embassy. Before I left Tokyo, he sent me a letter:

> This is to wish you success and happiness in your next assignment and those that follow. During these past eight years, you have played a significant part in recording pictorially most of the outstanding and historical events in the Pacific. I have been most favourably impressed by the seriousness and understanding you have displayed and by the effectiveness of your photography, which I have seen on the screen on so many occasions. We shall miss you at the various revues and functions which have taken the place of the earlier, grimmer scenes of the war. With best wishes.
>
> Sincerely, Douglas MacArthur.

Flickers of History

The last weeks were a blur of tedious arrangements for the move interspersed with sad farewells from friends. It was difficult to say goodbye to the Japanese cameraman, Kawaguchi, whom I had employed to help me cover the vast area under my jurisdiction. We had shared stories of the war, stories that were not dissimilar. He saw a lot of action as he covered the war from the Japanese side, and was lucky to survive after the Americans sank the Japanese destroyer on which he was travelling.

In 1950 Australia had no diplomatic representatives in Tokyo, so I had to arrange for our baby Patricia to be included on our passport. As she was born in a US hospital, she was considered an American citizen, which would make things difficult when we returned to Australia. Three weeks before we were due to leave, a haughty British diplomat told me it would take at least six weeks to complete the paperwork required to get her an Australian passport. He would not budge, so I exploded, telling him we would be on that ship, whether the passport was stamped or not. Patricia was an Australian, whether she was on the passport or not. In two weeks, the permission came through.

We were booked to sail on an old Burns Philp ship, the *Merkur*. With our belongings packed, our five Japanese servants lined up to say their tearful goodbye. By the end of it, we were all in tears. They had taken very good care of us all, particularly Patricia's amah, who would sit and talk to our baby for hours in Japanese. The amah was devastated when we announced we were leaving, because she had grown so attached to Patricia.

Part III: Occupation

The ship sailed out of Yokohama but before we got to our first stop in Kobe, Mary fell ill with an asthma attack. At Kobe, I had to ring MacArthur's office to ask for approval to get off the ship to take Mary to hospital. An army jeep was sent to pick us up and take us to the American hospital, while the children stayed on board the ship. It was a hair-raising ride to the hospital at top speed through the pelting rain. The driving seemed more dangerous than Mary's asthma. The hospital was ready for us and Mary was put straight into a wheelchair. At great speed, she was taken to the labour ward. The hospital staff had been told we were expecting a baby.

A night in hospital in the right ward did the trick for Mary and we returned to the ship. I carried her up the rickety gangway to a special deck cabin that was provided for her to rest in until we reached Hong Kong. When we arrived there, we had to wait two days for a heavy fog to lift before we could enter the port. As we were soon to discover, that delay was nothing compared to the other inconveniences experienced during the rest of the trip.

The ship was scheduled to take eighteen days to travel from Hong Kong to Australia. It took nine weeks! The Sydney office phoned through daily orders to the captain, who was forced to island hop down through the Pacific, to pick up every sort of cargo imaginable. Finally, the ship ran out of food and water and it was forced to stop in Rabaul to replenish the larder.

The port of Brisbane was a welcome sight. I left the ship there to fly down to Sydney to find accommodation before the family arrived. When I met the *Merkur*, I could see the family on the top deck, but our baby was nowhere to be seen. I yelled out, 'Where's Patricia?' and Mary went into a panic. When my family left the ship, with Patricia in tow, Mary explained the baby had contracted measles from another family, who had kept the whole thing quiet. Mary decided it was also best to keep Patricia's condition hidden and hide her below in the cabin, otherwise the ship would have been quarantined in Brisbane and nobody would have been allowed ashore.

As I helped them onto the dock, surrounded by the beautiful backdrop of Sydney Harbour, the scenes of war and occupation were replaced with thoughts of my new life and how I would fit back into Australia. I felt a sense of pride for the work that I had completed, and boosted by the telegram from my old boss, Ted Genock, in my top pocket, which read:

CONGRATULATIONS ON COMPLETION YOUR JAPANESE ASSIGNMENT STOP YOUR RECORD CONSISTENT NEWS AND QUALITY COVERAGE HAS RATED VERY HIGHEST LEVEL OUR WORLD REPORTING STOP BEEN SEEN FROM YOUR AUSTRALIA

BON VOYAGE
GENOCK

But I was already searching for the next story, which, when caught on film, could provide an audience with the same magic I had found in theatres since the beginning of the century. It was to be a new phase, not marred by the death and fear of war, but characterised by possibility and hope. It was time to concentrate on my family and my own country, but I knew the flickering images of the past would never leave me.

Epilogue

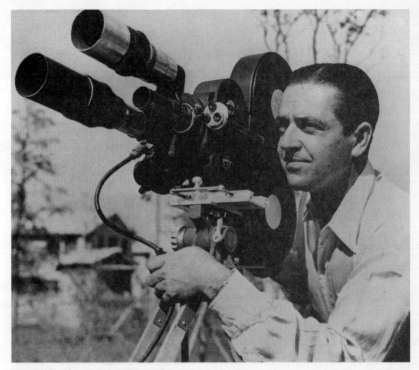

Bill Carty was Paramount News cameraman in Japan between 1945 and 1950. Here he is shown filming on the first day the Allied troops moved into Japan. Photograph: US Army Signal Corps.

EVERY YEAR WHILE IN JAPAN, I covered the annual peace ceremony held in Hiroshima. Every year I saw the city rise a little bit more from the ashes of the atomic bomb. Every year the ritual of setting free the doves became a little more elaborate. Every year the crowds of visitors who came to pay their respects increased, and the survivors looked a little older. When those survivors are gone from this world, all that will be left will be the memories.

Flickers of History

I remember a few families who lost husbands and sons in the First World War. I felt sorry for them, but I didn't really understand the impact of that war. For me, the threat of the Japanese invading Australia during the Second World War was much more real. In the same way, Hiroshima and Nagasaki will remain in my memory forever because I lived through those times.

When I first went to Japan, I hated the Japanese, as did most people in the Allied countries. I had seen evidence of some of the atrocities committed during the war. I soon came to realise, though, that the Japanese people, the children and the families, knew nothing about the actions of the Japanese Army. Their leaders kept the reality of the war a secret.

My feelings about Japan changed when I went to work and live there. One look at the Japanese children provided the first reminder that children are the same everywhere. We discovered the Japanese were kind and went out of their way to help their one-time enemy. My experience in Japan allowed me to gain a different perspective of the war, and, after living in that country, war did not seem so black and white.

Looking back over my career in motion pictures, fifty years is a lifetime.

I am the only cameraman left in Australia who began a career in the silent days of movies, then known as the flickers. The war created a different arena for the cameraman. All warcos took a risk just by being there. Some took more risks than others. Some were luckier than others. Those competing factors meant that some pictures were better than others, but it is pointless to say one cameraman was better than another. We

Epilogue

should all be recognised for carrying a camera, as those who were recognised for carrying a gun.

Of the many blessings I have enjoyed in my life, my marriage of sixty-three years to Mary Margaret is the most important, along with having had four lively children. The worst years of our married life came when I was away from home covering the campaigns, wondering all the time whether or not I would ever see my family again. The same feeling comsumed Mary. It was sheer hell when we were forced to separate for eighteen months in the last part of the war and the beginning of the occupation. Our faith and belief in God carried us through the rough times, and we believe God has been good to us. A chaplain once told me when I had come through an ordeal, 'It is your faith that will bring you through, and you, Bill, have that faith.'

The arrival of my family in Japan filled the emptiness I felt when we were apart for those long war years. For Jim and Helen, it was like the times in Sydney before the war, but the reconciliation was particularly important for Pauline and me, because I missed those first crucial years of her life. I wanted to make up for the lost time. Our fourth child, Patricia, who was born in Japan, was a real bonus for us.

Paramount gave me three months on full pay to adjust to Australia. At the end of that time, in June 1950, the Korean War broke out, and they asked me to return to cover it, but I declined with thanks. I was appointed chief news cameraman at Channel Seven, the second television station to move into Australia. After two years, my old employer, Cinesound Productions, offered me a job as film producer-director on documentaries. During that time, I produced and directed a film for BHP, called *Symphony in Steel*, which won four Australian film awards, including direction. I also produced two colour newsreels of Queen Elizabeth's visit to Australia in 1954. I moved on to become editor and produced Cinesound's two thousandth newsreel. When the company closed down the newsreels and merged with Fox Movietone several years later, I stayed on in the same position. I retired in 1973 after fifty years in the media, but my war footage lives on in a number of museums, including the Nimitz Museum in Texas.

When I retired from the industry, the motion picture world finished for me. I had no regrets leaving the work that I loved. Having the family together was more important to me.

I corresponded with Jean MacArthur, Bob Eichelberger, the Japanese cameraman Kawaguchi and many other friends until they died. I still write to Joseph Demers, the youngest member of the Montreal family that showed such kindness to me during the Depression. He is one of only three left of the eleven children in that family.

We have made several trips back to Japan since we left in 1950. That country and the poverty of the postwar era had a great effect on my son Jim, who became a missionary priest with the Marist order. He spent sixteen years in Japan, during which time he studied Japanese at the University of Tokyo for two years. He built the second refugee home in Japan and lobbied the Japanese government to allow boat people to stay while homes were found all over the world.

In my ninety-first year, I often read a speech that MacArthur gave on his seventy-fifth birthday, when he explained that

Epilogue

youth was a state of mind. He said it was not 'wholly a matter of ripe cheeks' but a temper of will, a quality of the imagination and a vigour of emotions. Nobody grows old by merely living a number of years, said MacArthur. Worry, doubt, self-distrust, fear, despair, pessimism and cynicism are the things which age us, while messages of beauty, hope, cheer and courage keep us young. I try to remember those sentiments.

Mary and I have had some wonderful years together. Neither of us know when our turn will come to leave this world. It will be a sad day for all of those families we leave behind, but we will have no regrets. The saddest day was when we lost Helen, our eldest daughter. Our consolation is that we believe that she is with God, and we hope to see her when our turn comes. My eyes now provide the only lens for me to see the world, and they flicker on to continue the search for the next story.